E S P A Ñ O L

¡EN VIVO!

INSTRUCTIONAL SPANISH WORKBOOK
FOR GRADES 4-8

LEVEL 2

SARAH ROWAN

Join our email list to hear about
special promotions and new publications!

info@envivopublications.com
www.EnVivoPublications.com
360-383-7002

Español En Vivo Instructional Workbook Level 2 for Grades 4-8

Credits:
Author: Sarah Rowan
Cover Illustration: Mary Frances Brown
Maps: Jeremy Davies

¡Bienvenidos!

About the Author

Sarah Rowan is currently the director and lead instructor at Salud Spanish Programs in Bellingham, WA.

Sarah has taught in many different settings, ranging from the school classroom to programs offered at her own Spanish language school. Besides teaching, she has been creating curriculum for children and adults for over 26 years.

Sarah received her M.A. in Spanish Literature at the University of Louisville, and has lived and traveled in Latin America and Spain.

About Español ¡En Vivo! Instructional Workbook Level 2

Español ¡En Vivo! Level 2 is the second workbook in the En Vivo instructional workbook series, offering a simple and realistic approach to learning the Spanish language while encompassing interesting cultural elements to which students can relate.

There are 5 units, and within each unit, there are 5 progressive lessons with dynamic spoken and written activities, allowing the students to practice in a fun and meaningful way. At the end of each unit, there is a review and a personal spotlight, highlighting lives of various kids throughout the Spanish-speaking world, with cultural and geographical details.

Enjoy **ESPAÑOL EN VIVO Level 2**!

Sarah Rowan
En Vivo Publications
www.EnVivoPublications.com
360-383-7002

Supplemental Digital Teacher Bundle is available at:
EnVivoPublications.com

¿Dónde se habla español?
Where is Spanish spoken?

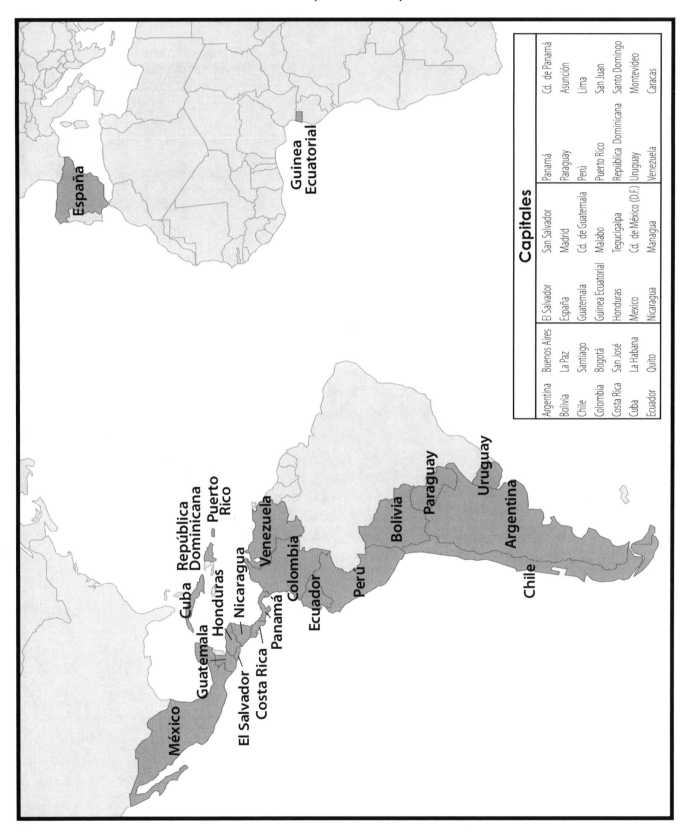

Capitales					
Argentina	Buenos Aires	El Salvador	San Salvador	Panamá	Cd. de Panamá
Bolivia	La Paz	España	Madrid	Paraguay	Asunción
Chile	Santiago	Guatemala	Cd. de Guatemala	Perú	Lima
Colombia	Bogotá	Guinea Ecuatorial	Malabo	Puerto Rico	San Juan
Costa Rica	San José	Honduras	Tegucigalpa	República Dominicana	Santo Domingo
Cuba	La Habana	México	Cd. de México (D.F.)	Uruguay	Montevideo
Ecuador	Quito	Nicaragua	Managua	Venezuela	Caracas

Índice / Table of Contents

PRONUNCIACIÓN

Letter	English sound		Examples
a	ah	f**a**ther	**mano** (hand), **cabeza** (head)
e	eh	m**e**t	**pez** (fish), **pelo** (hair)
i	ee	m**ee**t	**libro** (book), **gallina** (chicken)
o	oh	**o**pen	**oso** (bear), **mono** (monkey)
u	oo	sp**oo**n	**nublado** (cloudy), **azul** (blue)
h	--	*h is silent*	**helado** (ice cream), **hoja** (leaf)
j	h	**h**ot	**ajo** (garlic), **jamón** (ham)
ll	y	torti**ll**a	**silla** (chair), **estrella** (star)
ñ	ny	can**y**on	**España** (Spain), **araña** (spider)
rr	rr	*rr is "rolled"*	**perro** (dog), **gorra** (hat)
v	b	**b**at	**uva** (grape), **volcán** (volcano)
z*	ss	**s**at	**zanahoria** (carrot), **luz** (light)

* The "z" in Latin America sounds like an "s" while in Spain, it's pronounced with a "th" sound. This goes for "ci" and "ce" combinations, as well.

DIPTONGOS (Diphthongs)

A diphthong is a sound formed by the combination of two vowels. Try some of these! What do these words mean?

au ("ow")	**ai** ("ay")	**eu** ("eh-oo")	**ei** ("eh-ee")	**ie** ("ee-eh")	**ui** ("oo-ee")
auto	**ai**re	**Eu**ropa	r**ei**na	h**ie**lo	r**ui**do
j**au**la	b**ai**le	**eu**ro	ac**ei**te	n**ie**ve	c**ui**dado
fl**au**ta	v**ai**nilla	**Eu**genio	v**ei**nte	m**ie**l	b**ui**tre

UNIDAD

Mi vida diaria

My Daily Life

❖ Lección 1: Diálogos *(Dialogues)*

In En Vivo Level 1, you learned how to say hello and introduce yourself. Here they are again, along with a few more expressions added to the list.

Hola.	Hello.
Buenos días.	Good morning.
Buenas tardes.	Good afternoon.
Buenas noches.	Good night.
¿Cómo te llamas?	What is your name?
Me llamo...	My name is...
Mucho gusto.	Nice to meet you.
Igualmente.	Likewise.
¿Cómo estás? / ¿Qué tal?	How are you?
(Muy) bien.	(Very) well.
Regular. / Así así.	So-so.
Mal.	Bad.
¿Y tú?	And you?
¿De dónde eres?	Where are you from?
Soy de...	I am from...
Hasta luego. / Nos vemos.	See you later.
Adiós. / Chao.	Goodbye.

You also learned how to state your age, and whether you have siblings and pets:

¿Cuántos años tienes?	*How old are you?*
– **Tengo 10 años.**	*– I am 10 years old.*
¿Tienes hermanos?	*Do you have siblings?*
– **Tengo una hermana y**	*– I have one sister and*
dos hermanos.	*two brothers.*
¿Tienes una mascota?	*Do you have a pet?*
– **Tengo un perro y una gata.**	*– I have one dog and one cat.*

 **PRACTICAR** ———————————————————

1. Have a conversation with a partner, using pages 2 and 3 as a guide. Make sure you both have a chance to ask and answer the questions.

2. Your teacher will call out random questions and phrases. Write them down in the spaces provided, and come up with a logical response.

Teacher: Your response:

a. _____   _____

b. _____   _____

c. _____   _____

d. _____   _____

e. _____   _____

f. _____   _____

3. Make up three different dialogues, changing the phrases and order of questions. Once you're done, practice them with classmates.

Diálogo #1:

Persona #1: "_____" Persona #2: "_____"

Persona #1: "_____" Persona #2: "_____"

Persona #1: "_____" Persona #2: "_____"

Persona #1: "_____" Persona #2: "_____"

Persona #1: "_____" Persona #2: "_____"

Diálogo #2:

Persona #1: "_____" Persona #2: "_____"

Persona #1: "_____" Persona #2: "_____"

Persona #1: "_____" Persona #2: "_____"

Persona #1: "_____" Persona #2: "_____"

Persona #1: "_____" Persona #2: "_____"

Diálogo #3:

Persona #1: "_____" Persona #2: "_____"

Persona #1: "_____" Persona #2: "_____"

Persona #1: "_____" Persona #2: "_____"

Persona #1: "_____" Persona #2: "_____"

Persona #1: "_____" Persona #2: "_____"

 **ESCRIBIR** ———————————————————————

A. Complete the following dialogue exchanges with vocabulary and phrases from the previous pages.

1. Hola. ¿Cómo estás?   – _____

2. _____   – Me llamo Luis.

3. _____   – Tengo 11 años.

4. Mucho gusto.   – _____

5. ¿Tienes una mascota?   – _____

6. _____   – Sí, tengo 2 hermanas y un hermano.

7. ¿De dónde eres?   – _____

8. _____   – Bien, gracias.

9. ¿Qué tal?   – _____

10. ¡Adiós!   – _____

B. Make flash cards with this vocabulary, and practice with them at home. For the cards that contain questions, practice answering them, as well.

Sample:

Mucho gusto. *Nice to meet you.*	**Igualmente.** *Likewise.*
(Front)	*(Back)*

❖ Lección 2: ¿Cómo se escribe?
(How do you spell that?)

You've already learned the Spanish alphabet, but let's practice so spelling becomes automatic in your speech.

a	a	**ñ**	eñe
b	be	**o**	o
c	ce	**p**	pe
d	de	**q**	cu
e	e	**r**	ere
f	efe	**s**	ese
g	ge	**t**	te
h	hache	**u**	u
i	i	**v**	ve*
j	jota	**w**	doble ve*
k	ka	**x**	equis
l	ele	**y**	i griega, ye
m	eme	**z**	ceta
n	ene		

* In Spain, the "v" is pronounced "uve" and the "w" is pronounced "uve doble". Ask your teacher what he or she uses for these letters.

🗣 PRACTICAR

1. Write down the words your teacher spells out loud. If you need one repeated, say "Repita, por favor." ¿Qué significa? (What does it mean?)

a. _____ b. _____ c. _____

d. _____ e. _____ f. _____

2. With a partner, take turns spelling each of the words below while the other points to them. If you need the word repeated, say "repite, por favor". Then, ask, "¿Qué significa?" (What does it mean?)

mochila

rojo

gato

silla

verde

mesa

escritorio

tijeras

azul

cuaderno

papel

libro

✏️ ESCRIBIR ──────────────────────────

A. Write down 4 words in English you want to know how to say in Spanish. Look them up in the dictionary, and write the Spanish words in the blanks provided. Then, practice spelling them in Spanish.

English	Spanish		English	Spanish
1. _____	_____	3. _____	_____
2. _____	_____	4. _____	_____

B. Using a dictionary, if needed, write words containing the following letters, and practice the pronunciation. Consult the pronunciation key on page *iv* in the preface, as necessary.

1. **z** _____   *English:* _____

2. **ll** _____   *English:* _____

3. **j** _____   *English:* _____

❖ *Lección 3: ¿Cuántos hay?*
(How many are there?)

You're probably pretty good at counting in Spanish, but can you quickly say... **78** in Spanish? What about **536**? How do you say **9**?

1	uno	**15**	quince	**90**	noventa
2	dos	**16**	dieciséis	**100**	cien***
3	tres	**17**	diecisiete	**101**	ciento uno
4	cuatro	**18**	dieciocho	**200**	doscientos
5	cinco	**19**	diecinueve	**300**	trescientos
6	seis	**20**	veinte	**400**	cuatrocientos
7	siete	**21**	veintiuno*	**500**	quinientos
8	ocho	**30**	treinta	**600**	seiscientos
9	nueve	**31**	treinta y uno**	**700**	setecientos
10	diez	**40**	cuarenta	**800**	ochocientos
11	once	**50**	cincuenta	**900**	novecientos
12	doce	**60**	sesenta	**1.000**	mil
13	trece	**70**	setenta	**1.500**	mil quinientos
14	catorce	**80**	ochenta	**1.000.000**	un millón

* For the rest of the twenties, follow this pattern.   ** For 32-99, follow this pattern.
*** Cien is used only when it's exactly 100.

 PRACTICAR ──────────────────────────

1. With a partner, take turns rolling dice and saying the numbers out loud. Start with one die, and then try two, then three, and finally four!

Por ejemplo:

 dos

 sesenta y cinco

 quinientos quince

2. ¿Cuántas personas hay? Your teacher will call on someone to ask the question...

> **¿Cuántas personas hay en la fiesta?**
> (How many people are at the party?)

...and another student to answer the question based on the number s(he) writes on the board...

> **— Hay once personas en la fiesta.**
> (There are 11 people at the party.)

3. ¡BRINCA! Play this counting game with any number of people:

  a. Pick a number 1-9. This will be the *¡Brinca!* number, as well as any number containing that number or a multiple of that number.

  b. Start counting around the group with "uno," replacing the *¡Brinca!* number with the word *¡Brinca!*.

  c. The last one counting without making a mistake wins.

Por ejemplo: If the *¡Brinca!* number is 3...

  1–2– *¡Brinca!*–4–5–*¡Brinca!*–7-8-*¡Brinca!*-10-11-*¡Brinca!*-*¡Brinca!*-14, etc.

4. Ask several classmates what their phone numbers are. Jot down the numbers on a scrap piece of paper, and then confirm numbers.

¿Cuál es tu número de teléfono?

  — Mi número de teléfono es _ _ _ - _ _ _ _.

463-1972

Note: Try not to look at your book during this activity. Once you feel confident with single digits, try mixing in some double digits!

ESCRIBIR ————————————————————————————

A. Answer the following questions in Spanish.

1. ¿Cuántos años tienes? _____

2. ¿Cuántos minutos hay en una hora? _____

3. ¿Cuántas horas hay en un día? _____

4. ¿Cuántos días hay en un año? _____

5. ¿Cuántos años hay en un milenio? _____

6. ¿Cuántas sillas hay en la sala? _____

B. Solve the following math problems, writing out and saying the numbers out loud in Spanish.

+ más	**- menos**	**= son**

1. 2 + 3 = _____   4. 90 - 10 = _____

2. 300 + 600 = _____   5. 11 + 4 = _____

3. 50 - 30 = _____   6. 800 - 100 = _____

C. ¡LOTERÍA! Fill in each square with random numbers from 0-100 (use a pencil so you can change your numbers later), and play *¡Lotería!*

> **NOTE:**
> *Player that wins must call back their numbers in Spanish!*

❖ *Lección 4: Frases útiles en clase*
(Useful phrases in class)

A big part of communicating in class involves simple commands and questions. Let's learn and practice some!

Instrucciones y preguntas del maestro o de la maestra:

Saquen...	Take out...
... una hoja de papel.	... a piece of paper.
... el libro.	... the book.
... un bolígrafo/una pluma	... a pen.
... un lápiz.	... a pencil
Repitan.	Repeat.
¿Qué significa?	What does it mean?
Contesten en español.	Answer in Spanish.
¿Hay preguntas?	Are there any questions?
Escuchen (atentamente).	Listen (closely).
¿Entienden?	Do you all understand?
Escriban.	Write.
Cierren el libro.	Close the book.
Abran el libro.	Open the book.
Estudien.	Study.
Hagan la tarea.	Do the homework.
Lean en voz alta.	Read out loud.
Lean página(s)...	Read page(s)...

Frases y preguntas del/de la estudiante:

Tengo una pregunta.	I have a question.
Repita, por favor.	Repeat, please.
Más despacio, por favor.	Slower, please.
No sé.	I don't know.
¿Qué quiere decir...?	What does...mean?
¿Qué significa...?	What does...mean?
¿En qué página?	What page?
Con permiso.	Excuse me. *(Interruption)*
¿Puedo ir al baño?	Can I go to the bathroom?
(No) Entiendo.	I (don't) understand.
Perdón.	Excuse me. *(Sorry)*
¿Qué es esto?	What is this?
Gracias. / De nada.	Thank you. / You're welcome.
¿Cómo se dice...en español?	How do you say...in Spanish?

 PRACTICAR

1. Repeat the expressions on the previous 2 pages after your teacher, acting out any of them that are possible.

2. With a partner, take turns playing teacher and student, practicing these questions, commands and phrases.

 12   Español En Vivo Instructional Spanish Workbook Level 2 for Grades 4-8   ©2020 En Vivo Publications

3. In groups of 2-3 students, create a skit, using as many phrases from pages 11 and 12 as possible. After practicing it a few times, perform it in front of the class.

Personajes: _____   _____   _____
(Characters)

Lugar: _____
(Location - i.e. classroom, playground, cafeteria, etc.)

Fecha y hora: _____
(Date and Time)

_____
_____
_____
_____
_____
_____
_____
_____
_____
_____
_____
_____
_____
_____
_____

 **ESCRIBIR** ─────────────────────────

A. What would you say in Spanish in the following situations?

1. Your teacher is speaking very fast.

   _____

2. You want to ask your classmate how you say "table" in Spanish?

   _____

3. You don't know what page to go to in your book.

   _____

4. Someone asks you a question and you don't know the answer.

   _____

5. You need to interrupt two people in order to ask a question.

   _____

6. The teacher thanks you for erasing the board.

   _____

7. You accidentally dropped your book on your partner's foot.

   _____

8. You want to ask your teacher the meaning of "loco"?

   _____

B. Match the questions on the left with the logical answers on the right.

1. ¿Qué es esto? ___   a. No. Entiendo todo.

2. ¿Hay preguntas? ___   b. 83

3. ¿En qué página? ___   c. Es un reloj.

4. ¿Qué quiere decir "mochila"? ___   d. Significa "backpack".

❖ *Lección 5: Repaso* (Review)

A. Match the Spanish words with the English counterparts.

1. trece	____	a.	five hundred
2. página	____	b.	likewise
3. mochila	____	c.	thirteen
4. despacio	____	d.	desk
5. con permiso	____	e.	out loud
6. mucho gusto	____	f.	page
7. quince	____	g.	I don't know.
8. veinte	____	h.	Listen
9. baño	____	i.	you're welcome
10. libro	____	j.	backpack
11. igualmente	____	k.	red
12. No sé.	____	l.	slow
13. de nada	____	m.	question
14. quinientos	____	n.	excuse me
15. bolígrafo	____	o.	pen
16. Escuchen.	____	p.	nice to meet you
17. pregunta	____	q.	book
18. en voz alta	____	r.	fifteen
19. escritorio	____	s.	bathroom
20. rojo	____	t.	twenty

B. Walk around the room pretending like you don't know anyone. Greet and collect the following information from at least 3 classmates:

- Names and spelling
- How they are doing
- Age
- Phone numbers
- Number of siblings
- Number of pets

 Radiografía Personal ------------------>
Juan Costa Silva
11 años
La Habana, Cuba

A. Lee en voz alta. Read the following text out loud.

¡Hola! Me llamo Juan Costa Silva. Mi nombre se escribe J-U-A-N. Soy de La Habana, la capital de Cuba. Tengo once años y tengo dos hermanas, Marta y Susana. Me gusta mucho andar en bicicleta, a veces con mi perra, Lola. Ella es pequeña pero muy rápida. Mi hermana *menor*, Marta, *siempre me dice*, "¡Más

despacio!" Mi color favorito es el verde. Mi comida favorita es el *Congrí,* un *plato* típico de Cuba que consiste en arroz y frijoles. Mañana vamos a casa de mis abuelos en Moa. Bueno, ¡hasta luego!

Vocabulario:
menor - younger   **siempre** - always   **me dice** - tells me   **plato** - dish/plate

B. Contesta las preguntas. Answer the following questions about the text.

1. ¿Cómo se llama el chico? _____

2. ¿Cómo se escribe su nombre? _____

3. ¿De dónde es? _____

4. ¿Cuántos años tiene? _____

5. ¿Tiene hermanos?_____

6. ¿Tiene mascotas? _____

7. ¿Qué le dice su hermana menor cuando andan en bici? _____

8. ¿Cuál es su comida favorita? _____

9. ¿Y su color favorito? _____

10. ¿A dónde va Juan mañana? _____

C. ¡Ahora te toca a ti! It's your turn now! Use the text on the previous page as a model, and write about yourself in Spanish.

_____

_____

_____

_____

_____

_____

_____

_____

_____

_____

_____

D. ¿Quién es? The teacher will randomly collect some of the books and read the texts to the class, omitting the names. The class will then guess whose text it is.

UNIDAD

2

Los deportes y pasatiempos

Sports and Pastimes

❖ Lección 1: Los Deportes *(Sports)*

¿Qué te gusta hacer?
What do you like to do?

Me gusta...
I like to...

andar en bici

pescar

tocar el piano

jugar al fútbol

patinar

jugar al...	to play...	**andar en bicicleta**	to bike
... baloncesto	... basketball	**correr**	to run
... béisbol	... baseball	**esquiar**	to ski
... fútbol	... soccer	**hacer snowboard**	to snowboard
... fútbol americano	... football	**nadar**	to swim
... golf	... golf	**patinar**	to skate
... tenis	... tennis		
... voleibol	... volleyball		

 PRACTICAR ——————————————————

1. Practice saying the sports above with "Me gusta..." (I like...) and "No me gusta" (I don't like...) phrases, repeating after your teacher.

2. **¡CHARADAS!** Play charades with the various sports. To guess, you must say, "¿Te gusta...?"

Por ejemplo:
¿Te gusta jugar al béisbol?
(Do you like to play baseball?)
— ¡Sí, me gusta! *(Yes, I do!)*

3. Read each of the sports below out loud in Spanish, and then circle the one that does <u>not</u> belong. Be ready to state why.

ESCRIBIR

A. ¿Qué necesitas? What do you need in order to play the following activities? Follow the example given to complete the sentences.

un traje de baño   un casco   un bate

un balón   una pelota   una raqueta

Ejemplo: Para **jugar al fútbol**, necesito **un balón**.
To play soccer, I need a ball.

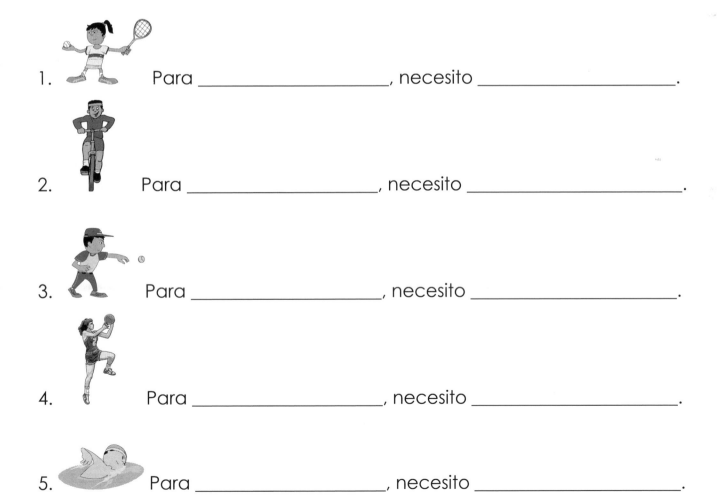

1. Para _____, necesito _____.

2. Para _____, necesito _____.

3. Para _____, necesito _____.

4. Para _____, necesito _____.

5. Para _____, necesito _____.

B. Complete the following crossword puzzle with the Spanish words for each of the clues in English.

CRUCIGRAMA (Deportes)

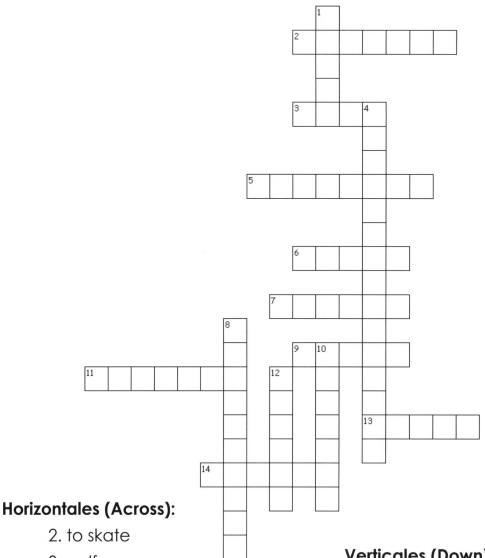

Horizontales (Across):

2. to skate
3. golf
5. volleyball
6. to play (a sport)
7. to run
9. tennis
11. baseball
13. to swim
14. ball (small)

Verticales (Down):

1. helmet
4. football (sport)
8. basketball (sport)
10. to ski
12. soccer

❖ *Lección 2: La Música* (Music)

¡Ojo!
Did you notice that "to play an instrument" is a different verb than "to play a sport" in Spanish?

tocar...	to play...
... la batería	... drums
... la flauta	... flute
... la guitarra	... guitar
... el piano	... piano
... el violín	... violin
cantar	to sing
escuchar música	to listen to music

¿Tocas un instrumento?
Do you play an instrument?

Sí, toco la guitarra.
Yes, I play the guitar.

 **PRACTICAR** ————————————————————————

1. a. Your teacher will state that (s)he plays various instruments. Repeat each one while acting like you're playing that instrument.
　　Por ejemplo:
　　　Toco el violín. *(I play the violin.)* - [Act out playing the violin.]

　　b. Now, your teacher will ask you if you play an instrument. Answer in a complete sentence.
　　　Por ejemplo:
　　　　¿Tocas el piano?　　— No, no toco el piano.
　　　　¿Cantas?　　— Sí, canto bien.

　　c. Finally, complete the table on the following page with information you gather after asking 2 classmates about their musical abilities.

　　It will go something like this:

　　　1. *You ask:*　　　　　**"¿Tocas el piano?"**
　　　2. *Classmate answers:*　　**"No, no toco el piano."**
　　　3. *You record:*　　　　Nombre: _(Melinda)_
　　　　　　　　　　　　_x_ No toca el piano.

　　Or:

　　　1. *You ask:*　　　　　**"¿Tocas la flauta?"**
　　　2. *Classmate answers:*　　**"Sí, toco la flauta muy bien."**
　　　3. *You record:*　　　　Nombre: _(Melinda)_
　　　　　　　　　　　　_x_ Toca la flauta...
　　　　　　　　　　　　(bien) / mal

Instrumento	Compañero(a) #1 Nombre: _____	Compañero(a) #2 Nombre: _____
	__ No toca el piano. __ Toca el piano... bien / mal	__ No toca el piano. __ Toca el piano... bien / mal
	__ No canta. __ Canta... bien / mal	__ No canta. __ Canta... bien / mal
	__ No toca _____. __ Toca _____... bien / mal	__ No toca _____. __ Toca _____... bien / mal
	__ No toca _____. __ Toca _____... bien / mal	__ No toca _____. __ Toca _____... bien / mal
	__ No toca _____. __ Toca _____... bien / mal	__ No toca _____. __ Toca _____... bien / mal
	__ No _____. __ _____... bien / mal	__ No _____. __ _____... bien / mal
	__ No _____. __ _____... bien / mal	__ No _____. __ _____.. bien / mal

¡Ojo!

You've now seen 3 different verb endings which tell us who the subject is :

Yo	toc**o**	I play
Tú	toc**as**	You play
Él/Ella	toc**a**	He/She plays

Here are a few more verb forms you can use...

| Nosotros | toc**amos** | We play |
| Ellos/Ellas | toc**an** | They play |

NOTE: There's a lot of power in Spanish verb endings, so much that you're not required to use subject pronouns.

Yo toco la batería. = **Toco** la batería   *I play the drums.*

 ESCRIBIR ───────────────────────────

A. Based on your findings in the previous table, make statements about similarities and differences of who plays which instruments. You may need to use the following words to link ideas:

y (and)   **pero** (but)   **también** (also)

1. Write down something that <u>both classmates do</u>. Indicate if they both do it well or if they both do it poorly.

   _____

2. Write down something that *Compañero(a) #1 does* but *Compañero(a) #2 does not*.

   _____

3. Write down something that *Compañero(a) #2 does* but *Compañero(a) #1 does not*.

   _____

4. Write down something that <u>you do</u> but that <u>one of your classmates does not</u>.

_____

5. Write down something that <u>one of your classmates does</u> but that <u>you do not</u>.

_____

6. Write down something that <u>both classmates do not do</u>.

_____

7. Write down something that <u>all three of you do</u>.

_____

B. Complete each sentence with the correct verb according to the subject.

1. Elena _____. (sings well)

2. Matt y Brian _____. (play the guitar)

3. Yo _____. (dance poorly)

4. Roger _____. (plays the drums)

5. Nosotros _____. (play the piano)

6. Tú _____. (play the flute)

7. Ellos _____. (listen to music)

8. Eva y yo _____. (play the violin)

❖ *Lección 3: Otros pasatiempos*

(Other Pastimes)

¿Qué quieres hacer?
(What do you want to do?)

— Quiero... *(I want...)*

acampar	to camp	**jugar a los videojuegos**	to play video games
bailar	to dance	**leer**	to read
cocinar	to cook	**pescar**	to fish
dibujar	to draw	**pintar**	to paint
ir al cine	to go to the movies	**tejer**	to knit
jugar a las cartas/ los naipes	to play cards	**ver la tele**	to watch TV

 PRACTICAR

1. Repeat the question "**¿Qué quieres hacer?**" after your teacher several times until you feel comfortable with your pronunciation. Then, your teacher will add a time reference to the questions. Repeat.

    ahora (now)   **esta noche** (tonight)

    mañana (tomorrow)   **este fin de semana** (this weekend)

2. Now, in pairs, take turns asking each other these questions and responding with real answers.

Por ejemplo: **¿Qué quieres hacer esta noche?** — Quiero estudiar.
(What do you want to do tonight?) (I want to study.)

✎ ESCRIBIR ─────────────────────

A. In Spanish, write 3 things you want to do and 3 things you do not want to do this weekend *(este fin de semana)*.

Este fin de semana...   **Este fin de semana**...

quiero... (I want to...)	**no quiero...** (I don't want to...)
1.	**1.**
2.	**2.**
3.	**3.**

B. Match the following activities you want to do in the first column with things you would need in order to do so. You may need to look some words up in the dictionary. Or ask your classmate or teacher, ¿Qué significa...? (What does...mean?)

1. Quiero dibujar. ____   a. Necesito un libro.

2. Quiero leer. ____   b. Necesito música.

3. Quiero cocinar. ____   c. Necesito una tienda de campaña.

4. Quiero acampar. ____   d. Necesito ingredientes.

5. Quiero bailar. ____   e. Necesito una caña de pescar.

6. Quiero pescar. ____   f. Necesito papel y un lápiz.

¡Ojo!

You're probably familiar with the verb forms **quiero** and **quieres** by now, so let's take a look at the other forms so we can talk about what other people want to do.

Yo	quier**o**	I want	toc**o**	I play
Tú	quier**es**	You want	toc**as**	You play
Él/Ella	quier**e**	He/She wants	toc**a**	He/She plays
Nosotros	quer**emos**	We want	toc**amos**	We play
Ellos/Ellas	quier**en**	They want	toc**an**	They play

Compare *querer* with *tocar,* which you just learned. Do they have anything in common? How are they different?

C. With a partner, compare your answers in **Actividad A** on the previous page. Then, write your partner's name in the blank, and complete the following table.

Este fin de semana, _____
compañero(a)

Este fin de semana _____
compañero(a)

quiere... (wants)	**no quiere...** (doesn't want)
1.	1.
2.	2.
3.	3.

D. Is there anything that both you and your partner want to do this weekend? Is there anything that you both don't want to do?

Por ejemplo: Tomás y yo **queremos** jugar al fútbol este fin de semana.
Thomas and I want to play soccer this weekend.

1. _____ y yo _____

2. _____ y yo no _____

❖ *Lección 4: ¿Qué vas a hacer?*
(What are you going to do?)

You just talked about what you want to do. Now, let's learn to express what you're **going to do** tonight, tomorrow and this weekend using the same verbs.

esta noche?
tonight

¿Qué vas a hacer...
What are you going to do...

mañana?
tomorrow

este fin de semana?
this weekend

- **Voy + a +**
I'm going to...

> nadar
>
> bailar
>
> cocinar
>
> jugar al fútbol
>
> dibujar
>
> ir al cine
>
> escuchar música
>
> leer
>
> estudiar

🗣 PRACTICAR ————————————————————

1. Repeat after your teacher as s(he) forms various questions and statements from the previous page. Then, your teacher will ask students questions about plans for **esta noche** (tonight), **mañana** (tomorrow) or **este fin de semana** (this weekend). Be prepared to answer!

2. With a partner, take turns asking what the other is going to do tonight, tomorrow and this weekend.

Por ejemplo: ¿Qué vas a hacer mañana?
                    — Voy a jugar al béisbol. ¿Y tú?

3. Take turns asking if the other is going to do something specific tonight, tomorrow or this weekend. Notice the **"Qué"** will disappear.

Por ejemplo: ¿Vas a estudiar esta noche?
                    — No, no voy a estudiar. Voy a escuchar música.

                ¿Vas a bailar este fin de semana?
                    — Sí, voy a bailar mucho.

4. Take turns asking your partner if he or she wants to do something, with **¿Quieres...?**

Por ejemplo: ¿Quieres estudiar conmigo *(with me)* esta noche?
                    — ¡Sí, quiero estudiar contigo *(with you)*! ¿Dónde?

ESCRIBIR —————————————————————————

A. First, take some time to review the various weather expressions you learned in *En Vivo Level 1*. Do you remember what they mean?

Hace frío.	**Hace calor.**	**Está lloviendo.**
Hace sol.	**Está nevando.**	**Está nublado.**
Hay un tornado.	**Hay una tormenta.**	**Hace viento.**

B. State what you're going to do based on what the weather is doing in the following drawings.

Por ejemplo: Hace frío. Voy a leer. (It's cold. I'm going to read.)

1. _____

2. _____

3. _____

4. _____

5. _____

6. _____

C. Write 3 things you're gong to do and 3 things you're not going to do this weekend.

Este fin de semana... | **Este fin de semana...**

voy a... (I'm going to...)	**no voy a...** (I'm not going to...)
1.	1.
2.	2.
3.	3.

¡Ojo!

The verb used in this expression is **IR** ("to go"). Notice how the verb forms don't resemble the infinitive:

Yo	**voy**	I'm going
Tú	**vas**	You're going
Él/Ella	**va**	He's/She's going
Nosotros	**vamos**	We're going
Ellos/Ellas	**van**	They're going

D. Interview a classmate about his or her weekend plans, and complete the following table with 3 things he or she is going to do and 3 things he or she is not going to do. You ask: **¿Qué vas a hacer este fin de semana?**

Este fin de semana, _____ | **Este fin de semana _____**
compañero(a) | compañero(a)

va a... (is going to...)	**no va a...** (isn't going to...)
1.	1.
2.	2.
3.	3.

❖ *Lección 5: Repaso (Review)*

A. Match the Spanish words with the English counterparts.

1. tocar ____	a.	bathing suit
2. baloncesto ____	b.	ball
3. patinar ____	c.	to play (an instrument)
4. pescar ____	d.	to dance
5. quiero ____	e.	weekend
6. cantar ____	f.	basketball
7. jugar ____	g.	volleyball
8. nadar ____	h.	you're going to
9. casco ____	i.	to skate
10. voleibol ____	j.	soccer
11. traje de baño ____	k.	drums
12. bailar ____	l.	to fish
13. fútbol ____	m.	helmet
14. cocinar ____	n.	guitar
15. cine ____	o.	I want
16. guitarra ____	p.	to cook
17. batería ____	q.	movie theater
18. vas a ____	r.	to sing
19. fin de semana ____	s.	to swim
20. pelota ____	t.	to play (a sport/game)

B. Walk around the room pretending like you don't know anyone, and have short conversations with at least 3 people. Include:

- Greet each other
- Ask if s/he likes to play any sports.
- Ask if s/he plays any musical instruments.
- Ask about plans tonight, tomorrow or this weekend using:
  ¿Quieres...? and **¿Vas a...?**
- Say goodbye.

Radiografía Personal ----------▸ Graciela Cuadra Sánchez
10 años
Montevideo, Uruguay

A. Lee en voz alta. Read the following text out loud.

¡Hola! Me llamo Graciela Cuadra Sánchez. Mi nombre se escribe G-R-A-C-I-E-L-A. Soy de Montevideo, la capital de Uruguay. Tengo diez años. Tengo un hermano que se llama Pablo. Me gusta mucho acampar. No hay montañas grandes en Uruguay pero hay muchos *bosques, lagos* y *ríos* muy bonitos. A veces, toco la

 guitarra *alrededor* de la *fogata*. También toco el piano pero ¡es imposible *llevar* un piano en mi mochila! Este fin de semana,

voy a acampar y nadar en un lago en el *monte* con mi familia. Bueno, ¡hasta luego!

Vocabulario:
bosque - forest   **lago** - lake   **río** - river   **alrededor** - around   **fogata** - campfire
llevar - to carry   **monte** - large hill

B. Contesta las preguntas. Answer the following questions about the text.

1. ¿Cómo se llama la chica? _____

2. ¿Cómo se escribe su nombre? _____

3. ¿De dónde es? _____

4. ¿Cuántos años tiene? _____

5. ¿Tiene hermanos?_____

6. ¿Qué le gusta hacer? _____

7. ¿Cómo es el paisaje en Uruguay?_____

8. ¿Toca un instrumento ella? _____

9. ¿Qué va a hacer este fin de semana? _____

10. ¿Con quién va?_____

C. ¡Ahora te toca a ti! It's your turn now! Use the text on the previous page as a model, and write your own Spanish text about yourself.

_____

_____

_____

_____

_____

_____

_____

_____

_____

_____

_____

_____

_____

_____

D. ¿Quién es? The teacher will randomly collect some of the books and read the texts to the class, omitting the names. The class will then guess whose text it is.

UNIDAD 3

Lugares en la comunidad

Places in the Community

❖ Lección 1: La Ciudad (City)

el banco	bank	**la oficina de correos**	post office
la biblioteca	library	**el parque**	park
el café	coffee shop	**la peluquería**	hair salon/barber shop
la escuela	school	**el restaurante**	restaurant
el hospital	hospital	**el supermercado**	grocery store
la iglesia	church	**el teatro**	theater
el museo	museum	**la tienda**	store

¿Dónde está el supermercado?
(Where is the grocery store?)

— Está en Avenida Rosales.
(It's on Avenida Rosales.)

 PRACTICAR ───────────────────────────

1. Your teacher will ask where various places are, saying "¿Dónde está...?" Point to it in the picture on the previous page, saying, "Aquí está." You can also state the street name, "Está en Calle 12." If it isn't in the picture, simply say, "No está aquí."

2. In pairs, take turns stating whether or not you would like to go to the following places. If you do want to go, indicate when.

Por ejemplo:

	Quiero ir al parque hoy.	*I want to go to the park today.*
or	**No quiero ir al parque.**	*I don't want to go to the park.*

1.

4.

7.

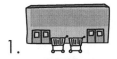
2.

5.

8.

3.

6.

9.

3. How often do you go to the following places? Use the following scale to complete this exercise. When done, read your statement out loud with a partner. How do your answers compare?

1 = Voy con mucha frecuencia
I go frequently

3 = No voy mucho
I don't go a lot

2 = Voy a veces
I go sometimes

4 = Nunca voy
I never go

1. ____ al hospital
2. ____ al parque
3. ____ a la peluquería
4. ____ al restaurante
5. ____ al supermercado

6. ____ a la escuela
7. ____ a la iglesia
8. ____ al banco
9. ____ a la biblioteca
10. ____ al teatro

Other expressions you can use:
todos los días - *every day*
demasiado - *too much*

de vez en cuando - *every once in awhile*
una vez a la semana - *once a week*
dos veces a la semana - *twice a week*

✏ ESCRIBIR

A. Match the following statements with the appropriate destination.

Voy...

1. Quiero ver arte. ____
2. Voy a comprar carne y arroz. ____
3. Me gusta aprender cosas nuevas. ____
4. Tengo el pelo demasiado largo. ____
5. ¿Quieres tomar un té conmigo? ____
6. Voy a mandar una carta. ____
7. Necesito dinero. ____
8. Necesito devolver un libro. ____

a. a la biblioteca
b. a la oficina de correos
c. al museo
d. a la escuela
e. al café
f. al banco
g. a la peluquería
h. al supermercado

B. Think about an area that you know well in your city or neighborhood, or a place that you like to visit out of town. Draw a map and label the places in Spanish.

❖ *Lección 2:* **Indicaciones** *(Directions)*

a la derecha (de)	to the right (of)	**enfrente de**	in front of
a la izquierda (de)	to the left (of)	**en la esquina**	on the corner
derecho/recto	straight	**a dos cuadras**	2 blocks away
entre	between	**al norte de**	to the north of
al lado de	next to	**al sur de**	to the south of
cerca de	close to	**al este de**	to the east of
lejos de	far from	**al oeste de**	to the west of

 PRACTICAR ─────────────────────────────────

1. With a partner, read the following question and answers out loud while flipping back to the picture on page 38.

> ***¿Dónde está la tienda?*** *(Where is the store?)*
>
> — ***Está al lado del café.*** *(It's next to the cafe.)*
>
> — ***Está a la izquierda del café.*** *(It's to the left of the cafe.)*
>
> — ***Está en la esquina de la Calle 12 y Avenida Rosales.***
> *(It's on the corner of 12th St. and Rosales Avenue.)*

2. Now, take turns asking each other where other places are in the picture. Answer in the same fashion, using the directional phrases.

¿Dónde está _____?   — Está _____.

3. The following verbs are useful when giving directions in Spanish. Practice them with your teacher.

seguir	to follow, "go"	➔	**Sigues...**	(You) go...
doblar	to turn	➔	**Doblas...**	(You) turn...
cruzar	to cross	➔	**Cruzas...**	(You) cross...

¿Dónde está la biblioteca? *(Where is the library?)*

— ***Sigues*** *derecho en la Calle Martín y **doblas** a la derecha en la Avenida Central. **Cruzas** el ferrocarril y la biblioteca está a la izquierda.*

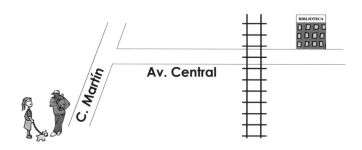

4. a. Take a moment to study the map of "Pueblo Hermoso" on the next page. Make sure you understand what all the establishments mean.

   b. Locate the starting point (**¡Estás aquí!**). Your teacher will give you directions to various places from this point. See if you can follow the directions and correctly state the final destination.

   c. In pairs, take turns doing the same activity, changing the destinations each time.

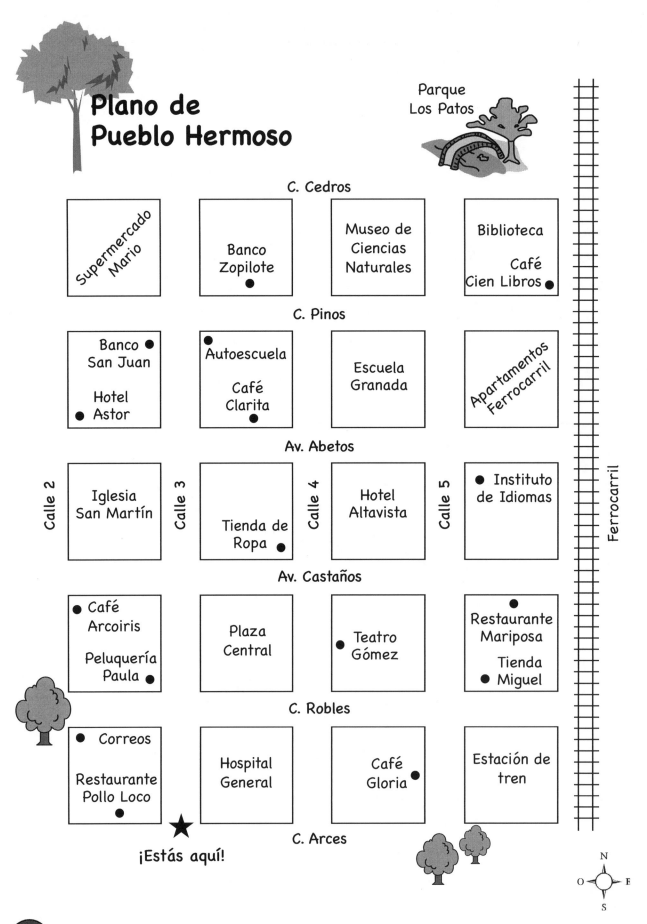

Plano de Pueblo Hermoso

Parque Los Patos

C. Cedros

Supermercado Mario

Banco Zopilote •

Museo de Ciencias Naturales

Biblioteca

Café Cien Libros •

C. Pinos

Banco • San Juan

Hotel • Astor

• Autoescuela

Café Clarita •

Escuela Granada

Apartamentos Ferrocarril

Av. Abetos

Calle 2

Iglesia San Martín

Calle 3

Tienda de Ropa •

Calle 4

Hotel Altavista

Calle 5

• Instituto de Idiomas

Ferrocarril

Av. Castaños

• Café Arcoiris

Peluquería Paula •

Plaza Central

• Teatro Gómez

• Restaurante Mariposa

Tienda • Miguel

C. Robles

• Correos

Restaurante Pollo Loco •

Hospital General

Café Gloria •

Estación de tren

★

¡Estás aquí!

C. Arces

N
O ✦ E
S

✎ ESCRIBIR ───────────────────────

A. Desde/A (From/To). Explain to a lost tourist in writing how to get to the following places:

1. Desde el **Supermercado Mario** al **Teatro Gómez...**

_____

_____

_____

2. Desde el **Café Cien Libros** a la **Tienda de Ropa...**

_____

_____

_____

3. Desde el **Restaurante Pollo Loco** al **Restaurante Mariposa...**

_____

_____

_____

4. Desde el **Café Arcoiris** al **Parque Los Patos...**

_____

_____

_____

❖ *Lección 3: ¿A qué hora?* *(What time?)*

¿A qué hora sale el tren?
What time does the train leave?

— El tren sale...
The train leaves...

... **a las** ocho.

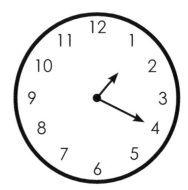

... **a la** una **y** veinte.

... **a las** cuatro **y media**.

... **a las** dos **menos cuarto**.

Notice that when stating times in Spanish you use...

- **a las** + hour, except when it's 1:00, in which case you use **a la una.**
- **y** after the hour when expressing the minutes after the hour.
- **menos** after the hour to express the minutes before the hour.
- **cuarto** to express a quarter (fifteen).
- **y media** to express half past the hour.

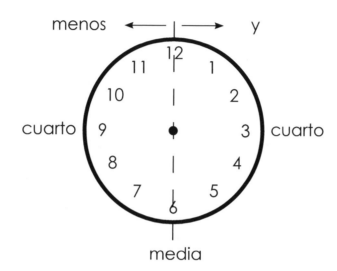

Other useful **time expressions**:

... a las dos **de la mañana**	at 2:00 *in the morning*
... a las tres y media **de la tarde**	at 3:30 *in the afternoon*
... a las diez y diez **de la noche**	at 10:10 *at night*
... al **mediodía**	at *noon*
... a **medianoche**	at *midnight*

🗣 PRACTICAR _____

1. State that you are going to the store at the following times below.

Por ejemplo: **3:10 p.m.**   Voy a la tienda **a las tres y diez de la tarde**.

2:00 p.m.	10:30 a.m.	8:00 p.m.
5:20 a.m.	3:45 p.m.	1:30 p.m.
12:00 p.m.	6:50 p.m.	9:10 p.m.

2. Your teacher will say that (s)he's going to various places around town at various times. For each one, complete the sentence and draw the clock hands with that time. Then, read the sentence out loud.

1. Mi maestro(a) va al/a la _____ a la(s)  .

2. Mi maestro(a) va al/a la _____ a la(s)  .

3. Mi maestro(a) va al/a la _____ a la(s)  .

4. Mi maestro(a) va al/a la _____ a la(s)  .

5. Mi maestro(a) va al/a la _____ a la(s)  .

ESCRIBIR ————————————————————————

A. Write out the following times in Spanish.

1. at 3:30 p.m. _____

2. at 2:00 a.m. _____

3. at 8:15 p.m. _____

4. at 1:10 p.m. _____

5. at 4:45 a.m. _____

6. at 9:20 a.m. _____

7. at 12:00 a.m. _____

8. at 6:40 p.m. _____

9. at 11:05 p.m. _____

10. at 12:00 p.m._____

B. State the time in Spanish that you typically do the following activities.

desayunar - to eat breakfast   **practicar** - to practice / to play
almorzar - to eat lunch   **hacer** - to do / to make
cenar - to eat dinner   **tener** - to have

1. ¿A qué hora desayunas típicamente? _____

2. ¿A qué hora almuerzas típicamente? _____

3. ¿A qué hora cenas típicamente? _____

4. ¿A qué hora practicas tu deporte favorito? _____

5. ¿A qué hora haces la tarea? _____

6. ¿A qué hora tienes la clase de español? _____

❖ *Lección 4: La Casa* (Home)

el ático

el dormitorio

la oficina

la cocina

el salón

el sótano

el garaje

¡Ojo!

The Spanish word **"casa"** means "house", but is frequently used for "home" as well:

Estoy en casa. *I'm at home.*
Voy a casa. *I'm going home.*

el ático	attic	**el jardín**	garden (flowers)
el baño	bathroom	**la oficina**	office
la cocina	kitchen	**el patio**	patio
el comedor	dining room	**la sala/el salón**	living room
el garaje	garage	**el sótano**	basement
la habitación*	bedroom	**la terraza**	deck, balcony
la huerta	garden (veggies)		

* There are several Spanish words for "bedroom", like **cuarto**, **recámara**, and **dormitorio**. Ask your teacher which one she or he uses.

 **PRACTICAR** ————————————————————

1. Ask your classmates what part of the house they like to do the following activities.

   Por ejemplo: ¿Dónde te gusta cantar? — Me gusta cantar en el baño.

leer	dormir	ver la tele
almorzar	trabajar	pensar en la vida
cocinar	tomar el sol	hablar por teléfono
estudiar	escuchar música	estar solo(a)

2. a. Write the Spanish word in the blank by the following household items. If you're not sure, ask a classmate or look it up in the dictionary.

bed _____	T.V. _____	chair _____
car _____	games _____	flowers_____
stove _____	sofa _____	refrigerator _____
book _____	milk _____	computer _____
clock _____	mirror _____	bathtub _____
box _____	stairs _____	table _____

   b. Respond where the items above are typically found in a house, as your teacher asks. Por ejemplo:

   ¿Dónde se encuentra un espejo?
   Where is a mirror found?

   — Se encuentra en el baño.
   It's found in the bathroom.

   c. Perform the same activity with a partner, taking turns asking and answering the question.

 **ESCRIBIR** ——————————————————

A. Tu casa de ensueño. Your family is moving to Santiago, Chile, and you've been asked to give input into the design of your new house. Sketch your dream house and label (in Spanish) the rooms as you would like to have them, including the kitchen, living room, bedrooms (no more than 3), bathroom, etc.

Mi Casa de Ensueño

B. **¿Dónde vas a...?** Match the rooms with where you're most likely going to do the following activities. You don't have to use all the rooms.

1. Voy a cocinar...   _____   a. ...en mi habitación.

2. Voy a estudiar...   _____   b. ...en el patio.

3. Voy a leer...   _____   c. ...en el baño.

4. Voy a limpiar...   _____   d. ...en el garaje.

5. Voy a jugar a las cartas...   _____   e. ...en la cocina.

6. Voy a dormir...   _____   f. ...en el jardín.

7. Voy a pintar...   _____   g. ...en el sótano.

8. Voy a escuchar música...   _____   h. ...en el salón.

C. Complete the following crossword puzzle with the Spanish words for each of the clues in English.

CRUCIGRAMA (Casa)

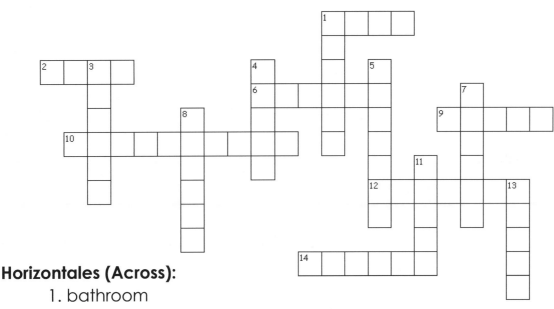

Horizontales (Across):
1. bathroom
2. table
6. mirror
9. living room
10. bedroom
12. office
14. kitchen

Verticales (Down):
1. bathtub   7. flower garden
3. basement   8. garage
4. clock   11. chair
5. dining room   13. attic

❖ *Lección 5: Repaso (Review)*

A. Match the Spanish words with the English counterparts.

1. kitchen	_____	a.	derecho
2. store	_____	b.	biblioteca
3. left	_____	c.	escuela
4. straight	_____	d.	baño
5. corner	_____	e.	cocina
6. dining room	_____	f.	garaje
7. church	_____	g.	lejos
8. right	_____	h.	izquierda
9. school	_____	i.	tienda
10. garage	_____	j.	iglesia
11. bathroom	_____	k.	derecha
12. far away	_____	l.	comedor
13. library	_____	m.	esquina

B. Give a classmate directions to the following places from your house:

1. tu parque favorito
2. la casa de un pariente
3. el supermercado
4. tu escuela

C. Ask your classmates the following questions in Spanish. Remember, the verb "to do" is **hacer**.

1. What are you going to do this weekend?
2. What do you want to do tonight?
3. What do you need to do tomorrow?

Radiografía Personal ------------------→ Ramón Rivas Leva
14 años
Colón, Panamá

A. Lee en voz alta. Read the following text out loud.

¡Hola! Soy Ramón Rivas Leva. Mis *apellidos* se escriben R-I-V-A-S L-E-V-A. Tengo catorce años y soy de Colón, Panamá. Colón se encuentra en un *extremo* del Canal de Panamá en el lado del Caribe. La Ciudad de Panamá es la capital de Panamá y está en el otro extremo del canal, del lado del Océano Pacífico. El Canal de Panamá es un *pasaje* de agua

que conecta el Océano Pacífico con el Océano Atlántico. Mis abuelos viven en Gamboa, un pueblo entre Colón y Panamá en la *selva*. Su casa es pequeña pero tiene todo lo que necesitan: una cocina, un baño y otro cuarto para dormir y ver la tele. Las casas en esta *zona* no tienen sótanos. Voy a visitar a mis abuelos este fin de semana para mi cumpleaños. El bus sale a las 3:00 de la tarde *en punto*, entonces necesito *hacer la maleta*. ¡Hasta luego!

Vocabulario:
apellido - last name   **extremo** - end   **pasaje** - passage   **selva** - forest/jungle
zona - area   **en punto** - sharp (time)   **hacer la maleta** - pack one's bag

B. Contesta las preguntas. Answer the following questions about the text.

1. ¿Cómo se llama el chico? _____

2. ¿Cómo se escriben sus apellidos? _____

3. ¿De dónde es? _____

4. ¿Cuál es la capital de Panamá y dónde está? _____

5. ¿Qué es el Canal de Panamá? _____

6. ¿Dónde viven sus abuelos? _____

7. ¿Cómo es la zona de sus abuelos? _____

8. ¿Cómo es la casa de los abuelos? _____

9. ¿Qué pasa este fin de semana? _____

10. ¿A qué hora sale el bus? _____

C. ¡Ahora te toca a ti! It's your turn now! Use the text on the previous page as a model, and write your own Spanish text about yourself.

_____

_____

_____

_____

_____

_____

_____

_____

_____

_____

_____

_____

_____

D. ¿Quién es? The teacher will randomly collect some of the books and read the texts to the class, omitting the names. The class will then guess whose text it is.

UNIDAD

¡Buen provecho!

Enjoy your meal!

> La comida está muy buena. ¡Quiero más!

> ¡Estoy lleno!

¡Ojo!

"Buen provecho" is the Spanish way of telling someone to enjoy his or her meal. If you ever come across someone who is eating, whether it be in a house, on the street or elsewhere, saying "buen provecho" is a polite gesture, as if to say, "sorry for the interruption, but carry on and enjoy."

If someone says this to you when you are eating, you can say, "gracias," and continue eating, and in some cases, it's even acceptable to offer the person some of your food.

❖ *Lección 1: En un restaurante*
(At a restaurant)

The following expressions are useful to know if you eat at a restaurant in a Spanish-speaking country.

Antes de pedir *Before ordering*	**Una mesa para dos, por favor.**	*A table for two, please.*
	El menú, por favor.	*The menu, please.*
	¿Qué me recomienda?	*What do you recommend?*
Para pedir *To order*	**Quiero sopa con ensalada.**	*I'd like soup with salad.*
	Para beber, quiero agua.	*To drink, I'd like water.*
	De postre, voy a probar el flan.	*For dessert, I'll try the flan.*
Durante la comida *During the meal*	**La sopa está muy rica.**	*The soup is very tasty.*
	Todo está muy bueno.	*Everything is delicious.*
	Necesito una servilleta.	*I need a napkin.*
Después de comer *After eating*	**La cuenta, por favor.**	*The check, please.*
	Gracias por todo.	*Thanks for everything.*
	Que tenga un buen día. **Que tenga una buena noche.**	*Have a nice day.* *Have a nice evening.*

🗣 PRACTICAR ─────────────────────────

1. Practice the phrases on the previous page with your teacher. Then, practice them with a partner, trying out variations, substituting different foods, etc.

2. a. Imagine you are at a Costa Rican restaurant, **Los Delfines**, looking at the menu on the following page. Your teacher will pretend to be the waiter and will ask you the following questions. How would you respond?

1. Buenas noches. ¿Una mesa para dos?

_____

2. ¿Para beber, qué quiere usted?

_____

3. ¿Y para comer? Le recomiendo el pescado.

_____

4. ¿Cómo está todo?

_____

5. ¿Toma usted algo de postre?

_____

6. ¿Quiere usted algo más?

_____

3. In groups of three, write a dialogue on a separate piece of paper between two customers and a waiter at **Los Delfines**. Use the expressions you just learned, as well as the same menu. Be prepared to present your dialogue to your class.

MENÚ

₡ = colones
₡ 1.000 = $1.85

— *Ensaladas* —

Ensalada mixta	₡ 1.000
Ensalada con pollo	₡ 1.500

— *Platos Principales* —

Pescado	₡ 5.000
Huevos fritos con arroz	₡ 4.200
Bistec con papas fritas	₡ 5.300
Pollo con salsa de mango	₡ 5.200

— *Postres* —

Helado – fresa, piña, mango y chocolate	₡ 400
Pastel de chocolate	₡ 750

— *Bebidas* —

Agua	₡ 250
Jugo – piña, mango, naranja	₡ 650
Café – solo o con leche	₡ 300

¡Gracias por su visita!
23 Av. Dos Piñas, Guápiles, Costa Rica
(506) 2241-4912

 ESCRIBIR ————————————————————————

A. ¿Cuánto cuesta? Practice your numbers by writing out in words how much the following menu items cost on the previous page.

1. El pescado cuesta _____ colones.

2. El jugo de naranja cuesta _____ colones.

3. El helado cuesta _____ colones.

4. El agua cuesta _____ colones.

5. La ensalada con pollo cuesta _____ colones.

6. Los huevos fritos cuestan _____ colones.

7. El pastel de chocolate cuesta _____ colones.

8. El café cuesta _____ colones.

¡Ojo!

As you know, the verb ESTAR is used to describe how someone is doing (bien, triste, nervioso, cansada, etc.). The two verb forms in bold are also used to describe how food tastes.

Estoy	I am
Estás	You are
Está	**It is** / He is / She is
Estamos	We are
Están	**They are**

Por ejemplo: El helado **está** muy bueno.

Los huevos **están** deliciosos.

B. Emparejar. Match the questions and responses between the waiter and customer in the most logical manner.

1. ¿Cómo están los tamales? ___   a. No, gracias. La cuenta, por favor.

2. Hola, bienvenidos a Los Pinos. ___   b. Le traigo una en seguida.

3. Necesito una servilleta. ___   c. Le recomiendo el pescado.

4. ¿De postre, quiere algo? ___   d. Están muy buenos, gracias.

5. ¿Cómo está la ensalada? ___   e. Hola. Una mesa para 2, por favor.

6. ¿Qué me recomienda? ___   f. Está muy rica, gracias.

7. ¿Desean algo más? ___   g. Quiero el pastel, por favor.

C. ¿Qué tal? Complete the following dialogues with the correct forms of *estar*.

1. MESERA: ¿Desean algo más?
   LUZ: Más sopa para mí. _____ deliciosa.

   • •   •   •   •   •   •   •   •   •   •   •

2. MESERO: ¿Qué tal todo?
   RAMÓN: Todo _____ buenísimo.

   • •   •   •   •   •   •   •   •   •   •   •

3. MESERA: ¿Cómo están los churros?
   JOSÉ: Horribles. _____ fríos y mojados.

   • •   •   •   •   •   •   •   •   •   •   •

4. MESERO: ¿Cómo está el pollo?
   SILVIA: _____ muy rico, gracias.

❖ *Lección 2: En el supermercado*

(At the grocery store)

Verduras

las zanahorias	carrots
la lechuga	lettuce
el maíz	corn
las papas/patatas	potatos
las cebollas	onions
los pepinos	cucumbers
los tomates	tomatos
los guisantes/ chícharos	peas
las habichuelas	green beans

Cereales

el arroz	rice
el pan	bread
la pasta	pasta
los cereales	cereal
la harina	flour

Carnes, Aves, Pescado

el jamón	ham
el pavo	turkey
el pollo	chicken
el cerdo	pork
el bistec	steak
la hamburguesa	hamburger
el pescado	fish

Frutas

los plátanos	bananas
las naranjas	oranges
las manzanas	apples
las peras	pears
las fresas	strawberries
las uvas	grapes
la piña	pineapple
la sandía	watermelon
los limones	lemons
los aguacates	avocados

Productos Lácteos

la leche	milk
el yogur	yogurt
el queso	cheese
el helado	ice cream
los huevos	eggs
la mantequilla	butter

 **PRACTICAR** ——————————————————————

1. Your teacher will pretend to be a customer and ask if there are certain foods in the grocery store:

Hola, buenos días. ¿Hay...?

You'll respond by indicating in which section each item is found:

Sí, hay... . Está(n) en la sección de...

2. Pretend you're going to make something for dinner. With a partner, list the items you need to buy at the grocery store, and see if he or she can guess what it is you're going to make. It will go something like this...

**Esta noche, voy a hacer algo para la cena.
Necesito lechuga, tomates, aguacate y zanahorias.**

Partner guesses: **¿Vas a hacer una ensalada?**

3. ¡LOTERÍA! Pick any 16 foods from the previous page and draw one picture of each in the squares below. Then, play **¡LOTERÍA!**

NOTE:
Player that wins must call back their foods in Spanish!

ESCRIBIR ──────────────────────────

A. Lista de compras. Make a grocery list for the following items you're going to make this week for dinner. Then, note the sections of the grocery store you will have to visit to find the items on your list.

LISTA DE COMPRAS

lunes	*martes*	*miércoles*	*jueves*	*viernes*
BURRITOS	HAMBURGUESAS	SOPA	ENSALADA	SALTEADO
1.	1.	1.	1.	1.
2.	2.	2.	2.	2.
3.	3.	3.	3.	3.
4.	4.	4.	4.	4.
5.	5.	5.	5.	5.
6.	6.	6.	6.	6.
7.	7.	7.	7.	7.
8.	8.	8.	8.	8.
POSTRE:	POSTRE:	POSTRE:	POSTRE:	POSTRE:

Secciones: Secciones: Secciones: Secciones: Secciones:

_____   _____   _____   _____   _____

_____   _____   _____   _____   _____

_____   _____   _____   _____   _____

_____   _____   _____   _____   _____

_____   _____   _____   _____   _____

* You may also need to visit these sections:
     Conservas - Canned foods   *Aceites y salsas* - Oils and sauces

B. Comparar. Compare your *lista de compras* with a classmate for each menu item. ¿Son parecidas? ¿Quién tiene la mejor lista?

¡Ojo!

You're familiar with the verb **NECESITAR,** as you expressed earlier what foods you *need* in order to make dinner. Here are some other useful verb forms:

Yo	necesit**o**	I need
Tú	necesit**as**	You need
Él/Ella	necesit**a**	He needs / She needs
Nosotros	necesit**amos**	We need
Ellos/Ellas	necesit**an**	They need

Notice the subject pronouns to the left of the verbs above. As you know, these are not grammatically necessary, as in English. However, they're useful when you want to emphasize the subject, as in...

Yo necesito cocinar.   I need to cook. (*Not* you.)

...or to distinguish between subjects, as in the case between él/ella and ellos/ellas...

Él necesita cocinar.   *He* needs to cook.
Ella necesita cocinar.   *She* needs to cook.

C. ¿Qué necesitas? In groups of three, compare your shopping lists, and complete the table below indicating the correct form of the verb ***necesitar,*** and what everyone needs to make the meals.

Para hacer burritos	Yo	Compañero(a) #1	Compañero(a) #2	Compañeros(as) #1 y #2	Nosotros
necesitar					
Comidas					

Para hacer sopa	Yo	Compañero(a) #1	Compañero(a) #2	Compañeros(as) #1 y #2	Nosotros
necesitar					
Comidas					

❖ *Lección 3: En el mercado*
(At the market)

¡Ojo!

El regateo is a cultural norm in most Hispanic open-air market places, where the customer and vendor haggle over the price of items being sold.

Since bargaining is not common in the U.S., many people feel uncomfortable, or even rude, offering a lower price for something being sold. Remember that in the Hispanic world, el ***regateo*** is expected, so don't think you're being inappropriate offering a lower price.

You'll notice that there's an art to effective ***regateo,*** being stern and pleasant at the same time. Have fun practicing it!

Cómo regatear

How to bargain

	El/La comprador(a) *(Buyer)*	**El/La vendedor(a)** *(Seller)*
Para saber un precio *To find out a price*	**¿Cuánto cuesta(n)?** **¿Cuánto vale(n)?** **¿A cuánto está(n)?** *(How much is it/are they?)*	**Cuesta(n)...** **Vale(n)...** **Está(n) a...** *(It/They cost(s)...[price].)*
Para reaccionar a un precio *To react to a price*	**Eso es mucho.** *(That's a lot.)* **Es demasiado.** *(That's too much.)* **Me parece muy caro.** *(That seems very expensive.)*	**No es mucho.** *(That's not a lot.)* **Es muy barato(a).** *(It's very cheap.)* **Está bien de precio.** *(It's a good price.)*
Para negociar *To negotiate*	**Le doy...** *(I'll give you...[price].)* **¿Qué le parece...?** *(How does [price] sound?)*	**Es muy poco.** *(That's very little.)* **¿Cuánto quiere pagar?** *(How much do you want to pay?)*
Para cerrar *To close*	**No, gracias.** *(No, thanks.)* **De acuerdo, le doy...** *(Ok, I'll give you [price].)*	**Este es el precio más bajo.** *(This is the lowest price.)* **Trato hecho.** *(Deal.)*

🗣 PRACTICAR ————————————————

1. With your teacher, practice the different bargaining phrases, from both the buyer's and the seller's viewpoints. Your teacher will point out some of the differences.

2. ¡El Mercado! Create a marketplace in your classroom!

You are in La Ceiba, Honduras, at a bustling outdoor market. Before following the instructions below, let's find out more about this area.

- ¿Dónde está Honduras?
- ¿Dónde está La Ceiba?
- ¿Cuál es la moneda *(currency)* de Honduras?
- ¿Qué productos se encuentran en un mercado hondureño?

a. Form groups of 2-3, according to your teacher's instructions. Each group will work on creating currency, will shop together and tend a market stand together.

b. Create currency you will be using at the market. Print out one sheet (10 bills per sheet) per denomination (1's, 5's, 10's and 20's) on different colored paper in order to visually distinguish the bills from one another.

c. In your group, set up a market stand with either pictures cut out from a magazine, empty packaging from home, or drawings of foods. Make price labels to place on them or write the prices directly on the items.

d. Your teacher will instruct your group to either stay at your stand to be the "vendedor(a)" *(seller)* or walk around and shop as the "comprador(a)" *(buyer)* or "cliente" *(customer)*. Use the table on the previous page to help you with your dialogue. Don't forget the polite greetings when you approach a stand or customer.

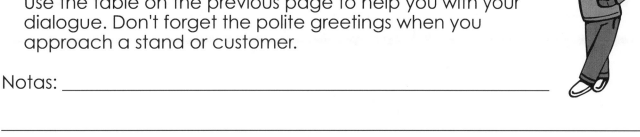

Notas: _____

_____

_____

_____

_____

 **ESCRIBIR** —————————————————————————

A. Emparejar. Match the questions or statements in the first column with a logical pair in the second column. Note: **L.** stands for Lempiras.

1. ¿Cuánto cuesta el pan? ___   a. Es muy poco. ¿L. 1.50?

2. ¿Le doy L. 11.00 por la bolsa. ___   b. Le doy L. 4.00.

3. Muy bien. Le doy L. 5.00 ___   c. ¿Cómo? ¡Es muy barato!

4. No, gracias. ___   d. Están a L. 3.00 por kilo.

5. Es demasiado. ___   e. Trato hecho.

6. ¿A cuánto están las papas? ___   f. Está bien. Tenga un buen día.

7. ¿Qué le parece L. 1.00? ___   g. Es muy poco. Está hecha a mano.

8. ¿Cuánto quiere pagar? ___   h. Cuesta L. 4.00. ¡Y está delicioso!

B. ¿A cuánto está? Unless you do the shopping in your family, you may not know what certain foods cost at the market. Ask your teacher, a parent or someone who knows general costs, and record the amounts below, using complete sentences.

1. ¿A cuánto están las papas? _____

2. ¿Cuánto cuesta un galón de leche? _____

3. ¿A cuánto está el kilo de salmón? _____

4. ¿Cuánto vale una zanahoria? _____

5. ¿Cuánto cuesta una barra de pan? _____

6. ¿Cuánto cuesta una lata de frijoles? _____

❖ *Lección 4: Los Sabores* (Flavors)

¿Cómo está la ensalada?
How does the salad taste?

— Está...

(muy) buena. *(very) good*

(muy) rica. *(very) tasty*

deliciosa. *tasty/delicious*

sabrosa. *tasty/delicious*

— Está...

(muy) mala. *(very) bad*

asqueroso(a). *disgusting*

horrible. *horrible*

LOS SABORES (flavors)		LAS TEXTURAS (textures)	
dulce	sweet	**suave**	smooth
salado(a)	salty	**blando(a)**	soft
agrio(a)	sour	**cremoso(a)**	creamy
amargo(a)	bitter	**crujiente**	crunchy
picante	spicy	**frío(a)**	cold
soso(a)	bland	**caliente**	hot

🗣 PRACTICAR

1. First, with your teacher, go over the pronunciation of the Spanish words for flavors and textures, as well as the names of the foods in the table below, and then continue to practice saying them with a partner.

2. With the same partner, see who can point to the food the fastest, as the teacher calls out either the food name or a description. Tally your points below and play to 10 (use a pencil so you can erase and play again).

Jugador(a) #1		Jugador(a) #2	
1	6	1	6
2	7	2	7
3	8	3	8
4	9	4	9
5	10	5	10

3. In pairs, take turns guessing the following adjectives while the other uses facial expressions as clues.

rico(a)   **crujiente**   **picante**   **agrio(a)**

frío(a)   **caliente**   **dulce**   **asqueroso(a)**

¡Ojo!

The verb **saber** means "to know", but it also means "to taste". To ask what something tastes like, you ask:

¿A qué sabe?

You respond: **Sabe a** *pollo.* (It tastes like chicken.)

Similarly, to ask what something smells like, you ask:

¿A qué huele?

You respond: **Huele a** *pollo.* (It smells like chicken.)

4. Bring 3 different foods and/or beverages from home for your partner to try blindfolded. For each item, ask your partner in Spanish, *¿A qué huele?* and *¿A qué sabe?*, while the partner responds, *Huele a* _____. and *Sabe a* _____.

	¿A qué huele?	¿A qué sabe?
Comida #1: _____	Huele a _____.	Sabe a _____.
Comida #2: _____	Huele a _____.	Sabe a _____.
Comida #3: _____	Huele a _____.	Sabe a _____.

Extra: ¿Cuáles son las texturas de las comidas?

¡Ojo!

Here are some important verbs that are frequently used when talking about food.

beber	comer	compartir
preferir	tomar	vender
comprar	probar	estar

What do they mean? Are you able to conjugate them? Review and practice them before completing the following exercises.

 ESCRIBIR —————————————————————————————

A. Seleccionar. Circle the adjectives that best describe the following foods.

1. Prefiero las zanahorias...

    a. picantes   b. cremosas   c. crujientes   d. saladas

2. El yogur es...

    a. cremoso   b. crujiente   c. caliente   d. picante

3. Los plátanos están...

    a. agrios   b. salados   c. crujientes   d. blandos

4. El helado está...

    a. amargo   b. frío   c. salado   d. agrio

5. Las fresas son...

    a. dulces   b. crujientes   c. sosas   d. saladas

6. ¿Tienes sal? La sopa está un poco...

    a. picante   b. fría   c. sosa   d. amarga

7. Este café está demasiado...

    a. blando   b. amargo   c. salado   d. picante

8. Las aceitunas son...

    a. saladas   b. cremosas   c. dulces   d. agrias

B. Traducir. Translate the following sentences from either English to Spanish or Spanish to English.

1. The chicken is hot. _____

2. The tacos are spicy. _____

3. Los plátanos están demasiado blandos. _____

4. Me gusta la crema de cacahuete crujiente. _____

5. Lemons are sour. _____

6. The soup tastes a little bland. _____

7. El café está muy amargo. _____

8. El pastel está demasiado dulce. _____

9. Olives are disgusting. _____

10. El jamón está salado. _____

C. Review the verbs on the previous page and then answer the following questions in complete sentences.

1. ¿Comes mucha comida dulce? _____

2. ¿Qué bebes durante la cena? _____

3. ¿Compartes tu postre con amigos? _____

4. ¿Tomas azúcar con el té? _____

5. ¿Pruebas muchas comidas diferentes? _____

_____

6. ¿Prefieres algo dulce o salado para el desayuno?_____

_____

7. ¿Comes pizza cuando está fría? _____

_____

8. ¿Compras crema de cacahuete cremosa o crujiente? _____

_____

❖ *Lección 5: Repaso* *(Review)*

A. Match the Spanish words with the English counterparts.

1. crujiente	____	a.	cheap
2. regateo	____	b.	delicious
3. harina	____	c.	disgusting
4. demasiado	____	d.	crispy, crunchy
5. necesitamos	____	e.	spicy
6. blando(a)	____	f.	rice
7. productos lácteos	____	g.	price
8. aguacate	____	h.	bargaining
9. barato	____	i.	avocado
10. dulce	____	j.	we need
11. pescado	____	k.	flour
12. precio	____	l.	turkey
13. amargo(a)	____	m.	dairy products
14. asqueroso(a)	____	n.	too much
15. picante	____	o.	fish
16. sabroso(a)	____	p.	soft
17. pavo	____	q.	bitter
18. arroz	____	r.	sweet

B. Take turns asking your classmates the following questions.

1. ¿Cuál es tu comida favorita cremosa? ¿...dulce? ¿...crujiente?

2. ¿Prefieres comer queso blando o duro?

3. ¿Cuál es tu comida menos favorita?

4. ¿Te gusta regatear? ¿Dónde regateas? ¿Eres bueno(a)?

5. ¿Necesitas cocinar de vez en cuando? ¿Qué cocinas?

6. ¿Cuál es tu restaurante favorito? ¿Qué pides?

RP Radiografía Personal ------------➤ Milu Chávez Morales
9 años
Tlaxiaco, México

A. Lee en voz alta. Read the following text out loud.

¡Hola! Soy Milu Chávez Morales y tengo nueve años. Vivo en Tlaxiaco, Oaxaca. Oaxaca es un *estado* en el sur de México donde hay mucha gente mixteca, uno de los muchos grupos *indígenas* de México. Mi nombre Milu es un nombre *mixteco* que significa "gato(a)" en español. Hoy estoy con mi familia en Ometepec, un pueblo a 4 horas de Tlaxiaco, visitando a mi abuelita. ¡Ella se llama Milu también! Ella tiene un *puesto* en el mercado donde vende frutas como piña,

mangos y plátanos. Toda la fruta está muy fresca y dulce. También vende sopa *casera*. Estoy comiéndola ahora mismo. ¡Está muy rica! Cuando alguien quiere comprar algo, muchas veces regatea con mi abuela, y mi abuela le dice con una *sonrisa*, "¡*Venga*! Usted sabe que está bien de precio." Pero todo el mundo siempre se va contento.

Vocabulario:
estado - state   **indígena** - indigenous/native   **puesto** - booth
casero(a) - homemade   **sonrisa** - smile   **¡Venga!** - Come on!   **se va** - leaves
mixteco - refers to the language of the indigenous group "la Mixteca"

B. Contesta las preguntas. Answer the following questions about the text.

1. ¿Dónde vive Milu? _____

2. ¿En qué parte de México está? _____

3. ¿Cuántos años tiene? _____

4. ¿A qué se refiere "mixteco"? _____

5. ¿Qué significa Milu en español? _____

6. ¿Dónde está Milu ahora? _____

7. ¿A qué se dedica su abuela? _____

8. ¿Qué comida hace su abuela para vender? _____

9. ¿Cómo está toda la comida? _____

10. ¿Se enoja la abuela cuando la gente regatea? _____

C. ¡Ahora te toca a ti! It's your turn now! Use the text on the previous page as a model, and write your own Spanish text about yourself.

_____
_____
_____
_____
_____
_____
_____
_____
_____
_____

D. ¿Quién es? The teacher will randomly collect some of the books and read the texts to the class, omitting the names. The class will then guess whose text it is.

UNIDAD

5

Los animales y su ambiente

Animals and their Environment

❖ *Lección 1: La Granja* (The Farm)

¿Qué hay en la granja?

What is there on the farm?

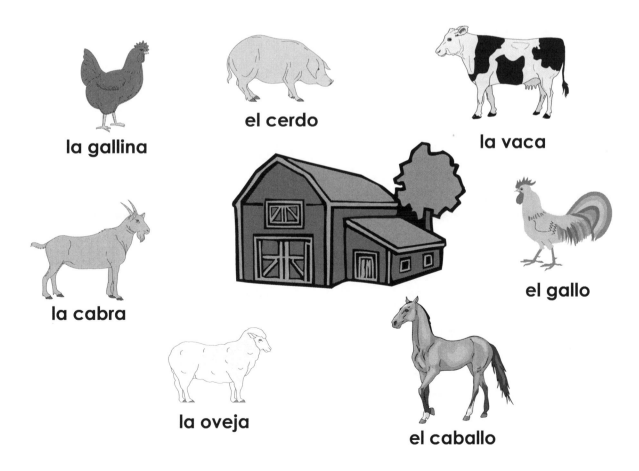

la gallina

el cerdo

la vaca

la cabra

la oveja

el caballo

el gallo

 **PRACTICAR**

1. Study the following animals, while saying them out loud. Then, play charades in small groups, as instructed by your teacher. Make sure you guess in Spanish. Por ejemplo: "¿Eres un gato? *(Are you a cat?)*

el burro	donkey	**el gato**	cat
el caballo	horse	**la oveja**	sheep
la cabra	goat	**el pato**	duck
el cerdo	pig	**el perro**	dog
la gallina	hen	**el pollito**	chick
el gallo	rooster	**la vaca**	cow

2. With a partner or in a small group, assigned by your teacher, play "20 preguntas" to try to guess the animal your classmate has selected.

Here are some possibilities:

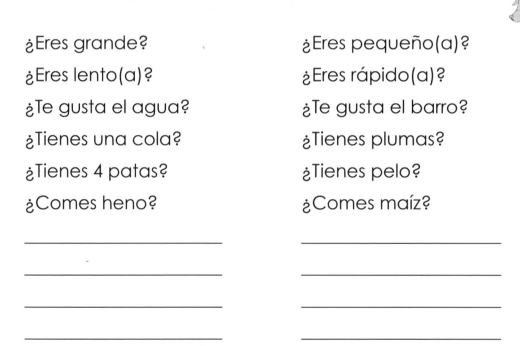

¿Eres grande?   ¿Eres pequeño(a)?

¿Eres lento(a)?   ¿Eres rápido(a)?

¿Te gusta el agua?   ¿Te gusta el barro?

¿Tienes una cola?   ¿Tienes plumas?

¿Tienes 4 patas?   ¿Tienes pelo?

¿Comes heno?   ¿Comes maíz?

_____   _____

_____   _____

_____   _____

_____   _____

ESCRIBIR —————————————————————————————

A. Draw a picture of your favorite farm animal.

B. Describe your animal now with words and state why it is your favorite animal. Exchange descriptions with a classmate for feedback.

_____

_____

_____

_____

_____

_____

_____

C. Place the farm animals from the previous pages into the categories below. Then, compare your results with a classmate.

Son más grandes que un perro	**No tienen pelo.**	**Son rápidos(as).**	**Les gusta estar con personas.**
_____	_____	_____	_____
_____	_____	_____	_____
_____	_____	_____	_____
_____	_____	_____	_____

D. Complete the following crossword puzzle with the Spanish words for each of the clues in English.

CRUCIGRAMA (La Granja)

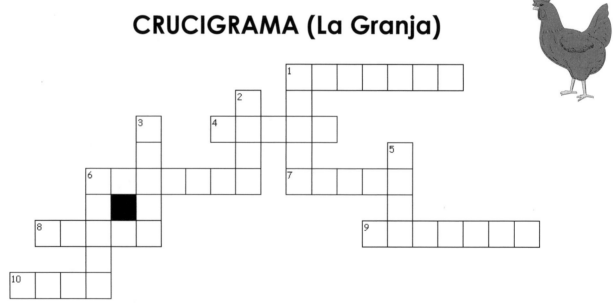

Horizontales (Across):
1. horse
4. goat
6. chick
7. sheep
8. donkey
9. hen
10. duck

Verticales (Down):
1. pig
2. cat
3. rooster
5. cow
6. dog

❖ *Lección 2: El bosque* (Forest)

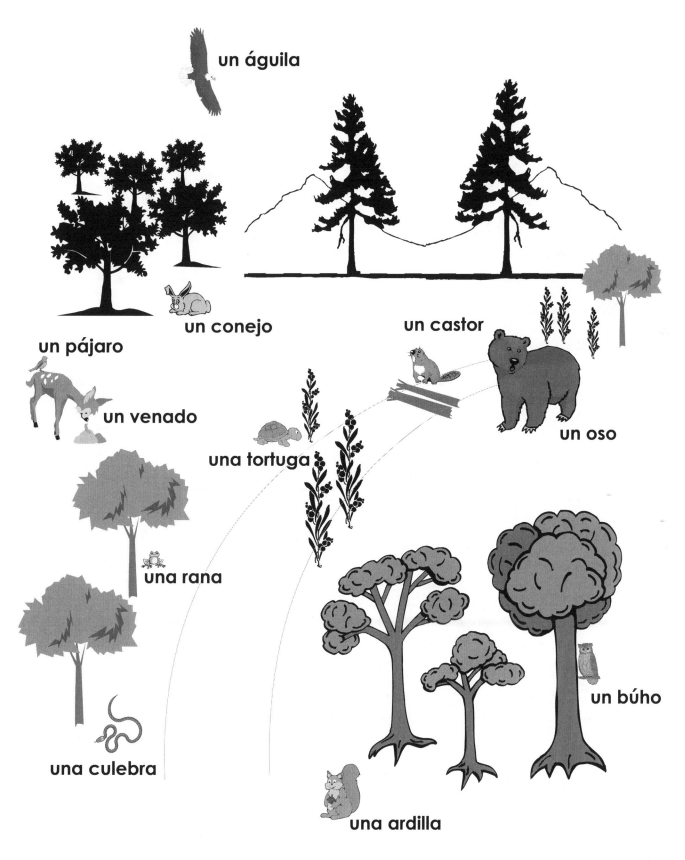

un águila

un conejo

un pájaro

un castor

un venado

una tortuga

un oso

una rana

un búho

una culebra

una ardilla

 **PRACTICAR**

1. Study the following animals, while saying them out loud:

el águila	eagle	**el lobo**	wolf
la araña	spider	**el mapache**	raccoon
la ardilla	squirrel	**el murciélago**	bat
el búho	owl	**el oso**	bear
el castor	beaver	**el pájaro**	bird
el conejo	rabbit	**el puma**	mountain lion
el coyote	coyote	**la rana**	frog
la culebra	snake	**la tortuga**	turtle
la hormiga	ant	**el venado**	deer

2. ¡LOTERÍA! Pick any nine animals from above and draw one picture of each in the squares below. Then, play **LOTERÍA**!

NOTE:
Player that wins must call back their animals in Spanish!

ESCRIBIR ――――――――――――――――――

A. Write the names of the animals in the appropriate categories. You may include farm animals, as well.

Tienen 4 patas.	Ponen huevos.	Viven en el agua.	Son salvajes.
1.	1.	1.	1.
2.	2.	2.	2.
3.	3.	3.	3.
4.	4.	4.	4.
5.	5.	5.	5.
6.	6.	6.	6.
7.	7.	7.	7.
8.	8.	8.	8.
9.	9.	9.	9.
10.	10.	10.	10.

B. Compare your lists with those of your classmates. Are they similar? Is there a category that does not contain any farm animals?

You're already familiar with the verbs **ser** and **estar**, and as you have seen, they are used in different situations. Let's review.

¡Ojo!

estar

yo	estoy
tú	estás
él, ella	está
nosotros(as)	estamos
ellos, ellas	están

To express the <u>temporary condition</u> of someone or something, or <u>location</u>, use **ESTAR**.

Ellos **están** tristes.   *They are sad.*
El gato **está** en el lago. *The cat is in the lake.*

ser

yo	soy
tú	eres
él, ella	es
nosotros(as)	somos
ellos, ellas	son

To express a <u>permanent</u> <u>quality</u> of someone or something, use **SER**.

Ella **es** alta.
Los leones **son** rápidos.

C. Fill in the blanks with the correct form of **<u>ser</u>** or **<u>estar</u>**, and then translate sentences into English.

1. Los mapaches _____ traviesos *(mischievous)*.

   English: _____

2. El oso _____ contento porque tiene comida.

   English: _____

3. Las ardillas _____ en el árbol.

   English: _____

4. La rana _____ nerviosa porque no hay muchas moscas para comer.

   English: _____

5. Los castores _____ ocupados con la construcción de su casa.

   English: _____

6. La culebra _____ muy larga y grande.

   English: _____

❖ *Lección 3: La sabana y la selva*
(Savannah and Jungle)

la cebra	zebra	la jirafa	giraffe
el chimpancé	chimpanzee	**el león**	lion
el cocodrilo	crocodile	**el loro**	parrot
el elefante	elephant	**el mono**	monkey
el gorila	gorilla	**el rinoceronte**	rhinoceros
el hipopótamo	hippopotamus	**el tigre**	tiger

🗣 PRACTICAR

1. On the next page, you will take the **¿Qué animal eres?** test, to determine what animal personality you are. Let's go over some of the verbs and vocabulary, in order to more effectively take the quiz.

practicar (to practice/play)		**llorar** (to cry)	
yo	practico	yo	lloro
tú	practicas	tú	lloras
él, ella	practica	él, ella	llora
nosotros(as)	practicamos	nosotros(as)	lloramos
ellos, ellas	practican	ellos, ellas	lloran
odiar (to hate)		**gritar** (to scream)	
yo	odio	yo	grito
tú	odias	tú	gritas
él, ella	odia	él, ella	grita
nosotros(as)	odiamos	nosotros(as)	gritamos
ellos, ellas	odian	ellos, ellas	gritan
hacer (to do/make)		**salir** (to go out/leave)	
yo	hago	yo	salgo
tú	haces	tú	sales
él, ella	hace	él, ella	sale
nosotros(as)	hacemos	nosotros(as)	salimos
ellos, ellas	hacen	ellos, ellas	salen
tener (to have)		**correr** (to run)	
yo	tengo	yo	corro
tú	tienes	tú	corres
él, ella	tiene	él, ella	corre
nosotros(as)	tenemos	nosotros(as)	corremos
ellos, ellas	tienen	ellos, ellas	corren
comer (to eat)		**vivir** (to live)	
yo	como	yo	vivo
tú	comes	tú	vives
él, ella	come	él, ella	vive
nosotros(as)	comemos	nosotros(as)	vivimos
ellos, ellas	comen	ellos, ellas	viven

veloz	fast	**natación**	swimming
fuerte	strong	**corredor(a)**	runner
valiente	brave	**caza**	hunting
aburrido(a)	boring	**carne**	meat
lento(a)	slow	**oscuridad**	darkness
divertido(a)	fun	**bosque**	forest
fácil	easy	**árbol**	tree

2. ¿Qué animal eres? Take the test below with a partner asking you the questions out loud.

¿Qué animal eres?

1. ¿Cómo es tu personalidad?

○ Soy veloz, fuerte y valiente. [**4**]

○ Soy aburrido(a), lento(a) e inteligente. [**1**]

○ Soy cruel y misterioso(a). [**3**]

○ Soy honesto(a) y muy divertido(a). [**2**]

2. ¿Qué deporte practicas?

○ Fútbol [**2**]

○ Corredor(a) [**3**]

○ Natación [**1**]

○ Caza [**4**]

3. ¿Qué haces cuando tienes miedo?

○ Nunca tengo miedo. [**4**]

○ Lloro y grito. [**2**]

○ Corro. [**1**]

○ No hago nada. [**3**]

4. ¿Te gusta la carne?

○ No. Soy vegetariano(a). [**1**]

○ No me gusta, pero la como. [**2**]

○ Sí, me gusta. [**3**]

○ Sí, me muero por ella. [**4**]

5. ¿Sales de noche?

○ No. Me asusta la oscuridad. [**1**]

○ Sí, pero sólo cuando es necesario. [**2**]

○ Me da igual. [**4**]

○ Sí. Adoro la oscuridad. [**3**]

6. ¿Dónde prefieres estar?

○ En el agua (mar, lago, río, piscina) [**3**]

○ En el bosque o en las montañas [**4**]

○ En un árbol [**2**]

○ En casa [**1**]

7. ¿Te gusta el trabajo?

○ No. Odio el trabajo. [**1**]

○ No, pero lo hago si es fácil. [**3**]

○ Sí, me gusta. [**2**]

○ Sí. Vivo por el trabajo. [**4**]

8. ¿Te gusta estar con otras personas?

○ No. Soy muy solitario(a). [**3**]

○ De vez en cuando. [**4**]

○ Sí, me gusta. [**1**]

○ Sí, necesito estar con otras personas. [**2**]

Suma los números arriba: _____
(Add the numbers above)

8-13	**jirafa**
14-19	**mono**
20-25	**cocodrilo**
26-32	**león**

Soy _____.

(Escribe el animal)

ESCRIBIR

You know a lot of adjectives already but let's learn how to compare things with them.

¡Ojo!

+   **más + adjetivo + que**

El león es **más rápido que** la cebra.
The lion is faster than the zebra.

-   **menos + adjetivo + que**

La jirafa es **menos ruidosa que** el mono.
The giraffe is less noisy than the monkey.

=   **tan + adjetivo + como**

El rinoceronte es **tan grande como** el hipopótamo.
The rhino is as big as the hippo.

A. Translate the following statements, using the correct comparative phrases above. Don't forget about adjective agreement!

1. The rhinoceros is more dangerous than the crocodile.   *peligroso*

   Español: _____

2. The chimpanzee is smarter than the zebra.   *inteligente*

   Español: _____

3. I am less strong than a gorilla.   *fuerte*

   Español: _____

4. The tiger is as big as the lion.   *grande*

   Español: _____

5. The elephant is heavier than the parrot.   *pesado*

   Español: _____

❖ *Lección 4: El Mar (Sea)*

Los animales del mar
Sea Animals

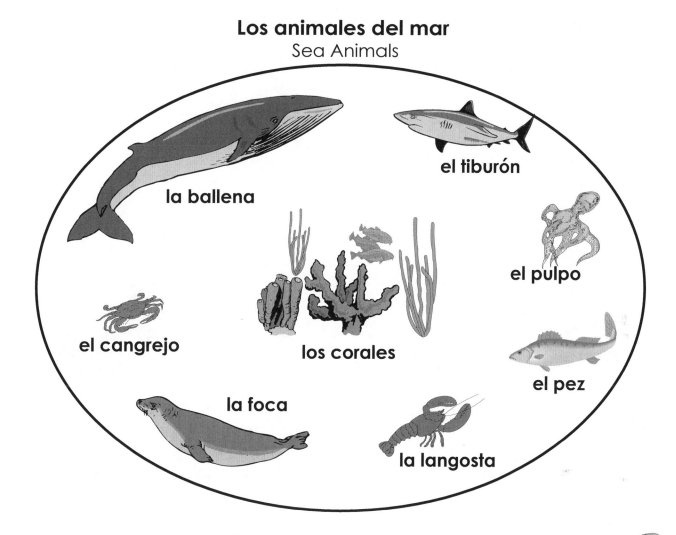

la ballena
el tiburón
el pulpo
el cangrejo
los corales
el pez
la foca
la langosta

la anguila	eel	**la medusa**	jellyfish
la ballena	whale	**el oso polar**	polar bear
el cangrejo	crab	**el pez**	fish
el delfín	dolphin	**el pingüino**	penguin
la foca	seal	**el pulpo**	octopus
la langosta	lobster	**el tiburón**	shark
el león marino	sea lion	**la tortuga marina**	sea turtle

🗣 PRACTICAR

1. **¿Qué ves?** You're scuba diving with a friend, and you see parts of the following animals.

Take turns asking each other what he or she sees: **"¿Qué ves?"**

Indicate what you think you see with: **"Veo un/una _____."**

1. 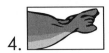 _____

2.  _____

3. 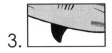 _____

4.  _____

5.  _____

6.  _____

7.  _____

8. 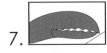 _____

2. ¿Qué animal es? Which animal is it?

a. First, do some research on a particular animal, without showing your classmates. Use these questions as a guide to obtain information, but add any other information you find interesting.

Mi animal es: _____

¿En qué parte(s) del mundo viven?   *¿Qué comen?*

¿Pasan todo el tiempo en el agua?   *¿Tienen aletas?*

¿Son grandes o pequeños(as)?   *¿Son peligrosos(as)?*

¿Caminan o nadan?   *¿Tienen dientes?*

_____

_____

_____

_____

_____

_____

_____

_____

b. After gathering your information and spending some time studying it, describe your animal in front of the class or your partner.

> **Note:** *All the verbs in the questions above are in the "ellos/ellas" form, asking about what "they" are like.*

When you finish your entire description, your class, or partner, will guess what animal it is.

ESCRIBIR

A. Follow the steps below to create your "Mónstruo del mar" (Sea Monster)!

Paso 1: Write any 5 numbers between 1-6 next to each body part.

	Cabeza
	Ojo
	Boca
	Brazo
	Aleta

Paso 2: Add an "s" to each body part that is next to a number greater than 1.

Paso 3: Draw a picture of your "mónstruo del mar" according to the specifications in your table in "Paso 1".

Paso 4: Present your "mónstruo del mar" to the class or in your group.

Por ejemplo: Mi mónstruo del mar tiene tres cabezas, dos bocas, y un ojo.

Mi Mónstruo del Mar

B. **¿Dónde se encuentran?** Write the Spanish names of the sea animals that correspond to the bubbles below. They may be used in more than one category. Compare your findings with your classmates.

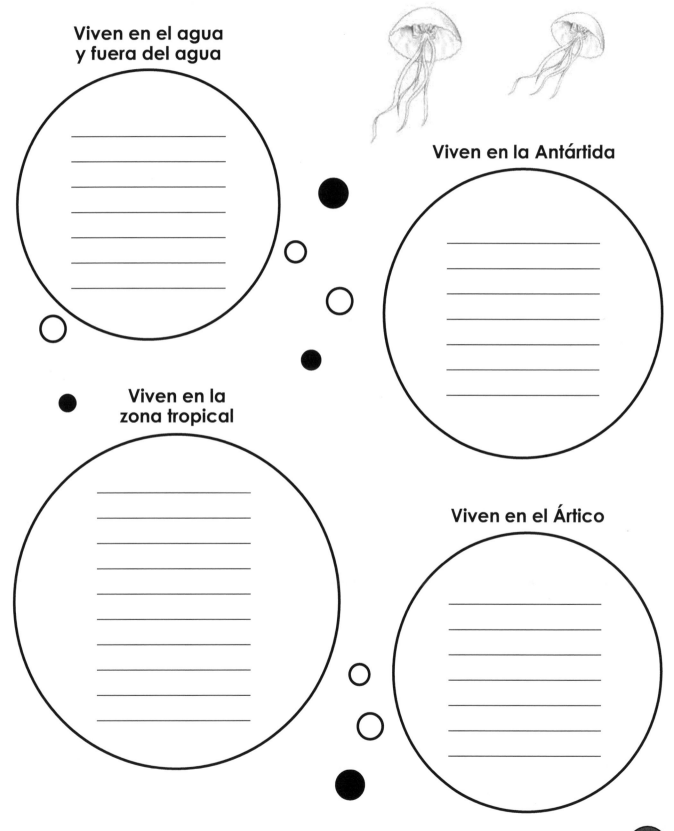

Viven en el agua y fuera del agua

Viven en la Antártida

Viven en la zona tropical

Viven en el Ártico

❖ *Lección 5: Repaso* *(Review)*

A. Match the Spanish words with the English counterparts.

1. conejo	____	a.	giraffe
2. jirafa	____	b.	sheep
3. rana	____	c.	turtle
4. tiburón	____	d.	raccoon
5. venado	____	e.	monkey
6. foca	____	f.	polar bear
7. oveja	____	g.	octopus
8. culebra	____	h.	horse
9. tortuga	____	i.	shark
10. pato	____	j.	duck
11. gallina	____	k.	wolf
12. oso polar	____	l.	ant
13. mapache	____	m.	rabbit
14. hormiga	____	n.	chicken
15. mono	____	o.	snake
16. lobo	____	p.	frog
17. caballo	____	q.	deer
18. pulpo	____	r.	seal

B. Translate the following sentences from English to Spanish.

1. The tiger is braver than the chicken. _____

2. Penguins live in Antarctica. _____

3. The deer is as big as the goat. _____

4. The frog is less intelligent than the raccoon. _____

5. Polar bears walk and swim. _____

6. Pigs don't have a lot of hair. _____

7. Sheep are less dangerous than sharks. _____

RP Radiografía Personal --------------------------> Berta
2 años
Vigo, España

A. Lee en voz alta. Read the following text out loud.

¡Hola! Me llamo Berta y soy una gallina gallega. Es decir, soy de Galicia, una provincia en el *noroeste* de España. Hablo *gallego*, el idioma de Galicia, y también el *castellano*, el español de España. El gallego es muy *parecido* al portugués. Vivo con mis hermanos, Susana, Frida y Carlos. Claro, Carlos es un gallo,

entonces *cacarea* mucho. No sé porque cacarean tanto los gallos. Tengo 2 años y ya *pongo muchos huevos*. Soy más inteligente que mis hermanos pero *no importa* mucho porque ellos encuentran *tantos* insectos *como* yo. Me gusta mucho comer, especialmente cuando Maricarmen nos da las *sobras* de la comida, como la lechuga y el arroz. Odio el pulpo (una comida muy típica en Galicia) pero lo comen mis hermanos. Mucha gente dice que llevo una vida aburrida, pero no es verdad. Paso mucho tiempo fuera del *gallinero*, corriendo por el campo, cazando insectos, *gusanos* y otros *bichos*. Tengo una vida muy divertida. ¡*Ata logo*!

Vocabulario:
noroeste- northwest ***parecido(a)***- similar ***cacarear***- to crow ***poner huevos***-to lay eggs
tantos como- as many as ***sobras***- leftovers ***gallinero***- coop ***gusanos***- worms
bichos- bugs ***no importa***- it doesn't matter ***¡Ata logo!***- ¡Hasta luego! in gallego

B. Contesta las preguntas. Answer the following questions about the text.

1. ¿Quién es Berta? _____

2. ¿Qué es una gallina gallega? _____

3. ¿En qué parte de España está Galicia? _____

4. ¿Qué idioma se habla en Galicia y cómo es? _____

5. ¿Con quién vive Berta? _____

6. Según ella, ¿qué hace Carlos frecuentemente? _____

7. ¿Qué hace Berta a los 2 años? _____

8. ¿Es ella inteligente? _____

9. ¿Cómo pasa el día? _____

10. ¿Es una gallina feliz? _____

C. ¡Ahora te toca a ti! It's your turn now! Use the text on the previous page as a model, and write your own Spanish text using another animal as the narrator and subject of the story.

_____

_____

_____

_____

_____

_____

_____

_____

_____

_____

_____

_____

_____

_____

D. ¿Quién es? The teacher will randomly collect some of the books and read the texts to the class, omitting the names. The class will guess who the person is.

Glosario

SALUDOS Y DESPEDIDAS (Greetings and Farewells) p. 2

Hola.	Hello.
Buenos días.	Good morning.
Buenas tardes.	Good afternoon.
Buenas noches.	Good night/evening.
¿Cómo te llamas?	What's your name?
Me llamo...	My name is ...
Mucho gusto.	Nice to meet you.
Igualmente.	Likewise.
¿Cómo estás?/¿Qué tal?	How are you?
(Muy) bien.	(Very) well, thanks.
Regular / Así, así.	So-so.
Mal.	Bad. / Sick.
¿Y tú?	And you?
¿De dónde eres?	Where are you from?
Soy de...	I am from...
Hasta luego./Nos vemos.	See you later.
Adiós./Chau.	Good-bye.

FRASES DEL/DE LA MAESTRO(A) (Teacher Phrases) p. 11

Saquen...	Take out...
... una hoja de papel.	... a piece of paper.
... el libro.	... the book.
... un bolígrafo/una pluma.	... a pen.
... un lápiz.	... a pencil
Repitan.	Repeat.
¿Qué significa?	What does it mean?
Contesten en español.	Answer in Spanish.
¿Hay preguntas?	Are there any questions?
Escuchen (atentamente).	Listen (closely).
¿Entienden?	Do you all understand?
Escriban.	Write.
Cierren el libro.	Close the book.
Abran el libro.	Open the book.
Estudien.	Study.
Hagan la tarea...	Do homework...
Lean en voz alta.	Read out loud.
Lean página(s)...	Read page(s)...

FRASES DEL/DE LA ESTUDIANTE (Student Phrases) p. 12

Tengo una pregunta.	I have a question.
Repita, por favor.	Repeat, please.
Más despacio, por favor.	Slower, please.
No sé.	I don't know.
¿Qué quiere decir...?	What does...mean?
¿Qué significa...?	What does...mean?
¿En qué página?	What page?
Con permiso.	Excuse me. *(Interruption)*
¿Puedo ir al baño?	Can I go to the bathroom?
(No) Entiendo.	I (don't) understand.
Perdón.	Excuse me. *(Sorry)*
¿Qué es esto?	What is this?
Gracias. / De nada.	Thank you. /You're welcome.
¿Cómo se dice...en español?	How do you say...in Spanish?

DEPORTES (Sports) p. 18

jugar al...	to play...
... baloncesto	... basketball
... béisbol	... baseball
... fútbol	... soccer
... fútbol americano	... football
... golf	... golf
... tenis	... tennis
... voleibol	... volleyball
andar en bicicleta	to bike
correr	to run
esquiar	to ski
hacer snowboard	to snowboard
nadar	to swim
patinar	to skate
el balón	ball (big)
el bate	bat
el casco	helmet
la pelota	ball (small)
la raqueta	racquet
el traje de baño	bathing suit

LA MUSICA (Music) p. 23

tocar...	to play...
... la batería	... drums
... la flauta	... flute
... la guitarra	... guitar
... el piano	... piano
... el violín	... violin
cantar	to sing
escuchar música	to listen to music

OTROS PASATIEMPOS (Other Pastimes) p. 28

acampar	to camp
bailar	to dance
cocinar	to cook
dibujar	to draw
ir al cine	to go to the movies
jugar a las cartas/los naipes	to play cards
jugar a los videojuegos	to play video games
leer	to read
pescar	to fish
pintar	to paint
tejer	to knit
ver la tele	to watch TV

LA CIUDAD (City) p. 38

el banco	bank
la biblioteca	library
el café	coffee shop
la escuela	school
el hospital	hospital
la iglesia	church
el museo	museum

la oficina de correos	post office
el parque	park
la peluquería	hair salon/barber shop
el restaurante	restaurant
el supermercado	grocery store
el teatro	theater
la tienda	store

LAS INDICACIONES (Directions) p. 42

a la derecha (de)	to the right (of)
a la izquierda (de)	to the left (of)
derecho/recto	straight
entre	between
al lado de	next to
cerca de	close to
lejos de	far from
enfrente de	in front of
en la esquina	on the corner
a dos cuadras	2 blocks away
al norte de	to the north of
al sur de	to the south of
al este de	to the east of
al oeste de	to the west of
seguir	to follow/continue
doblar	to turn
cruzar	to cross

LA HORA (Time) p. 46

a las ocho	at 8:00
a la una y veinte	at 1:20
a las cuatro y media	at 4:30
a las dos menos cuarto	at 1:45
de la mañana	in the morning (after time)
de la tarde	in the afternoon (after time)
de la noche	at night (after time)
al mediodía	at noon
a medianoche	at midnight

LA CASA (House) p. 50

el ático	attic
el baño	bathroom
la cocina	kitchen
el comedor	dining room
el garaje	garage
la habitación	bedroom
la huerta	garden (veggies)
el jardín	garden (flowers)
la oficina	office
el patio	patio
la sala/el salón	living room
el sótano	basement
la terraza	deck, balcony

EN UN RESTAURANTE (At a restaurant) p. 58

Una mesa para dos.	A table for two.
el menú	menu
¿Qué me recomienda?	What do you recommend?
Para beber, quiero...	To drink, I'd like...
De postre, voy a probar...	For dessert, I'll try...
La cuenta, por favor.	The check, please.
Gracias por todo.	Thanks for everything.

EN EL SUPERMERCADO (At the grocery store) p. 63

CEREALES	GRAINS
el arroz	rice
el pan	bread
la pasta	pasta
los cereales	cereal
la harina	flour

CARNES, AVES, PESCADO	MEATS, POULTRY, FISH
el jamón	ham
el pavo	turkey
el pollo	chicken
el cerdo	pork
el bistec	steak
la hamburguesa	hamburger
el pescado	fish

VERDURAS	VEGETABLES
las zanahorias	carrots
la lechuga	lettuce
el maíz	corn
las papas/patatas	potatos
las cebollas	onions
los pepinos	cucumbers
los tomates	tomatos
los guisantes/ chícharos	peas
las habichuelas	green beans

FRUTAS	FRUITS
los plátanos	bananas
las naranjas	oranges
las manzanas	apples
las peras	pears
las fresas	strawberries
las uvas	grapes
la piña	pineapple
la sandía	watermelon
los limones	lemons
los aguacates	avocados

PRODUCTOS LÁCTEOS	DAIRY
la leche	milk
el yogur	yogurt
el queso	cheese
el helado	ice cream
los huevos	eggs
la mantequilla	butter

EN EL MERCADO (At the market) p. 68

regatear	to bargain
el/la comprador(a)	buyer
el/la vendedor(a)	seller
¿Cuánto cuesta(n)?	How much is it/are they?
¿Cuánto vale(n)?	How much is it/are they?
¿A cuánto está(n)?	How much is it/are they?
Eso es mucho.	That's a lot.
Es demasiado.	That's too much.
Me parece muy caro.	That seems very expensive.
No es mucho.	That's not a lot.
Es muy barato(a).	It's very cheap.
Está bien de precio.	It's a good price.
Le doy...	I'll give you...
¿Qué le parece...?	How does... sound?
Es muy poco.	That's very little.

Glosario

¿Cuánto quiere pagar?	How much do you want to pay?
No, gracias.	No, thanks.
De acuerdo, le doy...	Ok, I'll give you...
Este es el precio más bajo.	This is the lowest price.
Trato hecho.	Deal.

LOS SABORES Y TEXTURAS (Flavors and Textures)   p. 71

¿Cómo está?	How does it taste?
(muy) bueno(a)	(very) good
(muy) rico(a)	(very) tasty
delicioso(a)	tasty/delicious
sabroso(a)	tasty/delicious
(muy) malo(a)	(very) bad
asqueroso(a)	disgusting
horrible	horrible
dulce	sweet
salado(a)	salty
agrio(a)	sour
amargo(a)	bitter
picante	spicy
soso(a)	bland
suave	smooth
blando(a)	soft
cremoso(a)	creamy
crujiente	crunchy
frío(a)	cold
caliente	hot

LOS ANIMALES DE LA GRANJA (Farm Animals)   p. 79

el burro	donkey
el caballo	horse
la cabra	goat
el cerdo	pig
la gallina	hen
el gallo	rooster
el gato	cat
la oveja	sheep
el pato	duck
el perro	dog
el pollito	chick
la vaca	cow

LOS ANIMALES DEL BOSQUE (Forest Animals)   p. 83

el águila	eagle
la araña	spider
la ardilla	squirrel
el búho	owl
el castor	beaver
el conejo	rabbit
el coyote	coyote
la culebra	snake
la hormiga	ant
el lobo	wolf
el mapache	raccoon
el murciélago	bat
el oso	bear
el pájaro	bird
el puma	mountain lion
la rana	frog
la tortuga	turtle
el venado	deer

LOS ANIMALES DE LA SABANA Y LA SELVA (Savannah and Jungle Animals)   p. 87

la cebra	zebra
el chimpancé	chimpanzee
el cocodrilo	crocodile
el elefante	elephant
el gorila	gorilla
el hipopótamo	hippopotamus
la jirafa	giraffe
el león	lion
el loro	parrot
el mono	monkey
el rinoceronte	rhinoceros
el tigre	tiger

VERBOS PARA CONJUGAR (Verbs to conjugate)   p. 88

practicar	to practice/play
odiar	to hate
hacer	to do/to make
tener	to have
comer	to eat
llorar	to cry
gritar	to scream
salir	to leave/to go out
correr	to run
vivir	to live

LOS ANIMALES DEL MAR (Sea Animals)   p. 91

la anguila	eel
la ballena	whale
el cangrejo	crab
el delfín	dolphin
la foca	seal
la langosta	lobster
el león marino	sea lion
la medusa	jellyfish
el oso polar	polar bear
el pez	fish
el pingüino	penguin
el pulpo	octopus
el tiburón	shark
la tortuga marina	sea turtle

ESPAÑOL ¡EN VIVO!
INSTRUCTIONAL SPANISH WORKBOOK FOR GRADES 4-8
LEVEL TWO

www.EnVivoPublications.com
360-383-7002